# Tunnel Vision

## A FOCUSED LIFE

*Carpe Diem!*

*Jan*

# Tunnel Vision
## A FOCUSED LIFE

*Isadora Fokine Beauregard*

**Tunnel Vision: A Focused Life**

Isadora Fokine Beauregard

F  I  R  S  T     E  D  I  T  I  O  N

Paperback ISBN: 9781939288585
Hardcover ISBN: 9781939288936
eBook ISBN: 9781939288943

Library of Congress Control Number: 2014938141

Cover Photo: James Fennell/The Interior Archive

Published by Beauregard Books, An Imprint of Wyatt-MacKenzie

ISADORA FOKINE BEAUREGARD

# TABLE OF CONTENTS

# Fireworks and Destructive Behaviors

*We acknowledge violence exists and choose to live without it. We find constructive ways to nurture children and families who have felt the harsh and devastating effects of abuse and trauma. We choose to practice therapeutic ways to promote a "Tunnel Vision" approach to healing troubled lives.*

This book is about what happened to me in the process of losing physical custody of my three young sons and one infant daughter. And then, how I empowered myself to create "substantial change in circumstance," to believe in myself, to follow a focused path and to allow miracles in. A girl from Greenwich, Connecticut fell madly in love with a charismatic dark handsome gentleman from Portofino, dancing under the starlit sky on a hillside in Hillsborough, California.

From the moment we met, I loved his air of simplicity, his passion for family, his joyful strong spirit and his ability to do the same thing day after day and make it appear extraordinary. He loved to cook extravagant meals; overwhelmed me with his blatant candor about life, his laughter and ability to maintain constraint over all material enticements. I recall he loved my mother dearly and honored her; I liked that. Though, I would come to comprehend the extent of his domineering character, the lengths to which he had to change me to his familiar "old world" ways.

My perception of reality as I knew it was built around a small-town upper-middle class image; my parents ran a thriving flower business. I was a model, a dancer and choreographer. We frequented upscale environments, Manhattan city lights. I shopped for the best. Rarely was I told no.

The story begins as my fear of who I was becoming grew. Mounting hostility in our relationship took over our ability to relax and simply relate to each other civilly. I lashed out emotionally to defend myself and justify my "way" rather than defuse his sarcasm. I ran from it, I hid from him. Attempts to medicate one child for asthma were met with resistance: "You are poisoning my children."

I was advised to run and hide rather than stay and deal with a situation I felt threatened by. Fleeing in the dead of night – what I thought was the only way out – turned out to be a decision with dire consequences, affecting the lives of many, causing me to lose my way, breaking up our marriage, and damaging my children for years to come. Perhaps I could have done more. I had not researched the Southern Italian culture; divorce was not common. Women subordinated to their husbands in all ways, or so I am told. In hindsight, I demanded to remain true to myself.

Though details of my life are to be minimized here as the benefit of telling my story is to help you, my journey forward has remained focused within tight imaginary walls – my "tunnel" – allowing me to maintain a sense of calm and self-control. I have suffered grief and hurt and felt immense pain from loss. I still do not believe I deserved what I went through. I shed enough tears so there are no more tears and I came to a decision to move on gracefully.

There is no time to stay in one place, no more pity party to be had. I had come to believe others would heal me. I believed justice would be done. I came full-circle to believe in myself, to love myself and my abilities. I came to realize everything will come from the way I think about things and the way I apply myself, taking action steps moving forward. With clear vision steeped in the knowledge that miracles are possible, I developed a concrete vision plan; no one could interfere, no words or negative energy could penetrate.

Adversity in life happens. If we do not allow it to take over our thoughts and actions we can decide deliberately to move forward positively. I pulled myself up by the bootstraps, took strength in the knowledge that silver linings appear when you least expect them; maintained flow, kept my own counsel. I took kindly to challenge, I stayed upbeat; I learn from lessons I was gifted! The truth is revealed in how we traverse our path. I walked, roller-bladed and ran daily. I maintained my children by my side. My competition came from within myself. Thoughts and images enlighten my way as I choose my thoughts and visions selectively; inspiration and guidance allow in calmness. Baby steps were taken starting from a small warehouse to a room in a house, to my own condo, to obtaining custody, to feeling okay about me and about us, loving my children totally and completely, owning our own farm. Further growth is inevitable! I completely believe in this process.

I invite you to allow miracles into your life. Believe totally in your abilities, enrich your passions, and never falter no matter what anyone else thinks about you. If others believe you crazy enough to climb insurmountable mountains, continue to climb of your own accord and reach a higher height. Never allow another to stop you or fault your path. With childlike devotion, continue onward one challenge after another, focus on your being, your values staying clear, committed and focused with total clarity on this unique difference in your being to rise above.

The rules I was told to live by, that surrounded and haunted me, telling me to stay away from my children, to move on and create "substantial change," attempted to hold me apart from them. I was not "the chosen parent" and therefore I should not act as though I was. I did not live by this philosophy. Somehow and in every way, I allowed myself to live by my own rules, I continued to enrich my life and the lives of my children with museums and theater performances. I surrounded myself with my children every second I was allowed. I shared my love, respect and honor with them every second of every day.

Therefore when you can and in any way you can allow your uniqueness to shine through. Love and honor yourself, embrace love, trust friends, be humble, be honest, want for less and achieve streamline focus within self-imposed limits which lead to your goals and aspirations. As I did, imagine yourself skipping gracefully one challenge after another, saying "I think I can" and "go for it" to reach beyond previously imposed limits. Decide you will create amazing harmony from this imaginary place of peace from within. This healing guide– I gift to you.

I empower you now with love, kindness, and awareness. This methodology reveals how the most negative, confining, and challenging of events can become amazing and precious opportunities to grow if we open our eyes and embrace each moment. Love for Self as a unique and worthy individual will allow you to overcome hurdles, to emerge victorious. Open the door to your soul; write your story from your own perspective compassionately; be moved by this moment and share your joys and your sorrows. Allow your words to touch your soul fully, then you will see what you must do in ways suited to your life; heal yourself!

Perhaps you have been overwhelmed, misguided, stuck in a rut, traveled down a path leading nowhere, not certain where to turn. Perhaps life has served you up a curveball and you have forgotten how to respond. Perhaps you are unfamiliar with your surroundings, lacking passion in your way and need to gently refocus your energies and commitments. Perhaps you give all of your energy away to others to the point there is no energy left. It is within your power NOW to awaken body, mind and spirit to make change happen.

Believe me, it is within your power to uncover immense inner strength. Open yourself like a beautiful rose, petal by petal, uncovering all of you in all your uniqueness. Explore riches within you– mirror them back, sharing all of you with another in expressions of kind words, a gentle touch – telling another how much they mean to you to move their spirit. Every day I told my amazing children how much I adored them. "Mom, you are the best mom ever for listening."

I share this story from the bottom of my heart. I promise if you follow healing lessons you will benefit. I am a natural healer. I have overwhelmingly committed to the lightness of spirit, heart; to mentor health, happiness, and humility from a perspective of someone who thrives on, joyfully and passionately experiencing all good in this life. I am not without fault and I share this too. Still, I am capable of great passion, to laugh fully, to share my experiences with excitement. Life is not a dress rehearsal; when the curtain rises the audience appears to take in the show! I take the stage, prepared to excel, overjoyed at the opportunity to shine. I am blessed to have had the ability to take advantage of life's opportunities. I will never look back to doubt myself. I will keep moving on, seeing beauty in the little things.

I make known to all professional doctors, psychologists, and judicial counsel the factual and circumstantial evidence to state my case. This book is written for those affected by harsh and sometimes inhumane decisions of the court. It is written for judges and juries who make decisions. Each factual scenario is seen in the eyes of the beholder, no misrepresentation to cause prejudice and condemnation. All are innocent until proven guilty. Each of us must be seen from a position of strength.

Whether you are a victim of circumstance or a victim of your own conscience, I pray my words can serve some gentle guidance for you. This healing methodology – "Tunnel Vision" – may provide encouragement. After all is said and done, there is a happy ending if you will this to be so. Demand it, as my one son said, "Mom fight for me." I had no choice but to succeed. Amazing what conviction can do! All of my lovely and loving children have become bright, caring successful individuals whose lives are filled with promise, traveling well beyond the trials of the past. They harbor no doubt and they carry in their psyche respect and dignity for both of us parents despite some chaos they were made to endure. All is as perfect as one would imagine – now dancers, dreamers, and entrepreneurs.

I have regret for some decisions in my life. I see in my friends patience to give and take graciously without having to bolt. I am filled with humility for a bright future ahead. I have climbed many mountains and plan to climb more as I am sticking to a plan. At the helm of my boat, I am in command of my destiny, never faltering from this vantage point. I invite you to join me to dream big and move on. I pray this epiphany becomes a vehicle of change, encouragement, love, courage, and empowerment to light your way! Tunnel Vision Approach is a stepping stone to forge new beginnings. Allow this roadmap to be so revealed.

Make a decision to take charge, to hold no one else accountable, to solidify a foundation for growth, to aspire to change for the better. I purposely drew away from the comments, judgments, and perceptions of others to create my special space to direct focus calmly and intentionally. My mantra, "An Architecturally Perfect Tunnel" with artistic boundaries to define the best starting point from which to create miracles and never look back. I was meant to thrive, I was meant to enjoy life, to accomplish whatever I set out to accomplish. I have accomplished sons and one beautiful daughter, I purchased a farm, obtained my MBA, completed law school. My creative side yet inspires a love for landscape architecture and gourmet cooking. You too must enjoy life! Celebrations take place, miracles unfold as they should.

I am graced with the ability to have actualized the momentum of my methodology. Whatever I set to accomplish was actualized though many along the way said it could never be and actually created through their negative energy walls of doubt. I pledge to give back to you knowledge, experience, and guidance with humor steeped in reality. I became stronger from this journey when I stopped listening to the negativity along the way. I embrace the power from within to forgive and forget a past that bound me to limitations of thought and action. I pray for those in my past who haunted and held me back. I send out healing love as this too is freeing. I utilize lessons from the past, insight provided by my actions. Perhaps I could have responded to my situation differently, precious life lessons to embrace. Each day is an opportunity to embrace the moment. Carpe Diem!

I assist you to find ways to awaken passions, to make change happen from deep within as you feel and experience. Do not allow any other person to tell you what you can and cannot become. Whether they call you crazy for your climb to overcome adversity, take pleasure in knowing you are okay! Take this moment to honor yourself! I will assist you to live in dynamic flow, to be mindful of our time here, to blame no one but yourself, to empower greatness in yourself each step of the way. Never stop believing in who or what you are no matter the obstacles in your path. Write, read, exercise, embrace life, accepting the twists and turns of fate with honor and allow yourself to breathe. Whatever the roadmap, all experiences are provided to shape our lives never more than we are capable of handling. I was meant to experience all that was placed in my path so that I may share this story with you today. I am moved by others who experienced greater life challenges than I.

I reach from within myself to find reasons for things rather than to seek out others to blame! Every day is but an opportunity to embrace my "now" and make a difference. Do not hold to what you cannot change, do not spend life wounded by your past or to seek to find revenge. To play a violin or to sing a sad song becomes boring and redundant. It is more interesting to take risks, to challenge the pain, to move on to experience life even if you falter.

Therefore, grab roller blades, a kayak, enjoy friends, purchase a farm, invest in olive trees, go to school, love, live a little and sponsor an orphan! The roller coaster will naturally allow for up and down motion to stay on the track as around and around it goes. So we learn from our ability to allow for and to thrive with freedom of movement, even with the most terrifying and uncomfortable movements of our lives. Allow others to be as they are; do not restrict the flow of their natural being. My children taught me best how to get along with my ex exactly as he is. They were much more adaptable than I ever was.

I thank friends who cried with me and held me close. It meant so very much that you genuinely cared during those times and took time to listen. Do not hide from feelings and emotions of your life. Allow others to share these times and take time to speak about things as it is best not to bottle up emotion. After a while, great healing will come if you allow it to be so and you let it go. As you allow healing in you will soften; share your emotional journey as I have done. My story, not unlike many before this, weaves a web of humanity to allow for others to be as they are, to love fully and passionately. I cannot imagine a more full life! I am a better person for it.

My son Cedric's ability to express himself in the courtroom was key to his ability to gain freedom from feeling like a "caged animal." He did not falter, he demanded of himself and of me to "go for it." I was told to fight harder for him. Something in the determination of the moment, there was no choice but to win. We moved on as if we had already won – a strong feeling.

Trials in life are a gift, to be embraced courageously to allow the creation of miracles! I acknowledge anything is possible if you set your mind to it. Good thoughts can enrich a day. A warehouse can become a country estate! I can be the nurturing babysitter if I set my mind to this task. I can expand my horizons. My list continues and I expect many miracles moving forward.

I encourage you to make a list; reflect, grow, embrace change from within the confines of wherever you find yourself. My warehouse became my "castle." I strive to share life lessons with you to make each and every lesson useful. Do not let the insanity of the moment upset the beauty of your being. Exercise your body with attention to every detail! Eat healthy foods from the garden to keep strong and vigorous! Surround yourself with friends who support your growth without judgment. My three sons and one adorable daughter are my constant guides, always loving, always believing. I am honored by their presence. Even when I became fearful, they stayed strong. "Mom, get in, get out, get on with it!"

No matter how complicated your story, stay steadfast, stand strong, believe and move forward. The transcendence of your personal roadmap including detours and setbacks is paramount. Then, allow for miracles big and small. Draw pictures; take photographs; allow in all good thoughts. My farm looks and feels much like the warehouse! When success comes as it will for certain, celebrate and continue on with a fearless attitude. Trust yourself and follow your heart. Acknowledge and embrace goals openly. Security breeds confidence, dreams are had and you will heal. Believe this to be so and things will unfold as they should.

If you are immobilized by loss and fear, there is a way out of your present state, a way to shape forward motion gracefully. Decide at once to transform your being, allow growth and accept change naturally with a focused path. It is easier if you keep on this way. The Tunnel Vision Approach is not about perceptions of pain and suffering. It not about a violin playing or a pity party heaped upon you by past misfortunes. It is forward looking, naturally causing positive things to happen.

The change you aspire to has nothing to do with creating sympathy or wallowing in grief. No emoting or wasted time allowed. The train you are on is moving in forward motion. The straight narrow focus is a dynamic strategy; clarity of purpose, disciplined thought, focused tomorrows and new beginnings key. One solid course of action forged, secure, steadfast, determined from here forward. Go for it!

Paint a picture in your mind's eye, enjoy this backdrop! Draw in whatever color, in whatever medium to suit your fancy. When I imagine a perfect tunnel, I image green landscapes, garden paths, lined with amazing plantings, curving naturally past olive and fig trees, a calming influence which sways and nurtures me onward. See this image: fresh, alive, and fun-filled with no influence or judgment from another. Never change from your focus if this is what you seek; whatever others believe is not important. Nurses went on strike nine times the past two years demanding rights. I am healed caring for patients so I stay honored to care. A father comes up to me crying saying I made the difference for their family during this time.

I began each day in silent prayer, the power of peace and love for my little ones; the belief in myself. Calmed by divine guidance my Tunnel Vision provided a focus with no room for distraction. This methodology assisted me to take the next step without looking back, mindful of the task at hand, not questioning the past. I call to spirits to lighten my path, secure in action, self-induced completion drives me onward. Joy of the quest is clear. Together now, we march onward – you and I – single-minded in focus, purposeful and intentional. I travel on and so can you; there is much left to be done. And miracles happen as I see them everywhere. I beckon you to join me on the creation of a journey all your own. You must believe: "Mom, fight for me, you are not fighting hard enough." I had no choice but to win.

Climb every mountain lest you will get left behind. Do not stop to listen to idle chatter of others for they have no knowledge of your quest. I assure you that if you provide the time to explore all that is wrong with your endeavor or seemingly "reaching for the stars" there are those who will find fault in the plan! Reach your personal fulfillment, no one else's plan. The guide that matters is with you. Support is there as it was for me if you simply believe this to be so. Do not surrender to the mind's wanderings nor idle chatter to sway you or drown out your ability to accomplish goal attainment. Make every moment count in each day; choose to have clarity of vision. Silver Linings are everywhere dressed in clouds of confusion, doubt, lack of conviction and others negativity. Push all that aside and welcome in the light! I came to see silver linings in all things; I looked for and sought them out. I turn my attention to good always. Never stop believing in miracles.

# Once Upon a Time

*There exist new and creative ways to successfully cushion lives surrounded by violence. There are ways to speak, to act and to focus in order to promote positive energy flow and to enjoy a healthier and less troubled post-trauma life. A learned behavior pattern, "Tunnel Vision" is utilized to reduce the likelihood of the perpetuation of trauma. Self-empowerment, brought about by consistent nurturing and loving support backed with a disciplined imagination and focus, will lead to a more stable and violence-free life.*

The warehouse would have been unimaginable just months prior. My home was a big, comfortable, immaculate one in California. My husband was tall, dark, handsome and worldly, our four children were stunningly beautiful and healthy. Our Swedish au pair looked after them. I can't seem to shake the memory of a day – though there were many like it – with my babies and me and the au pair out in the sun-drenched solarium, the two older boys (four and two-and-a-half, the youngest of the boys just six months), and my daughter seventeen months capturing the colors outside with the brightest crayons in their box. I don't know why I think of that day. Maybe because of how it juxtaposes with the times shortly ahead of it.

After I was denied physical custody of my children by the Court and with no money to my name, a complete stranger, having heard my plight, was kind enough to offer me the room. It wasn't much, she'd said, just a few square feet in the back of a warehouse, behind a rented farmhouse in the countryside where horses grazed free. I took it with gratitude. I made it light and beautiful; it became my Italian oasis.

There was no hot water in the warehouse, and a well capacity of just about five gallons of cold water for a shower. Funny, I remember this so well! No kitchen; I improvised, using a rice cooker to prepare a combination of vegetables, when I could afford them, from a close-by roadside stand. My friend Carole brought dinner on occasion, rolled sandwiches and juice after our exercise class. We would watch *Philadelphia*, hang out, laugh, and occasionally shed some tears. It became our retreat of sorts for me and close friends. While living in the warehouse, St. Gregory's Church provided me an opportunity to connect with wonderful people and offered us rations of bread and muffins. We embraced this opportunity to pray.

The events that led me from that sun-drenched solarium in my beautiful home in Saratoga to the tiny room in the cold warehouse were staggering and debilitating, almost paralyzing. Even now, it's hard to imagine I could have recovered; I would ultimately come to view this warehouse as a sanctuary; it would become the place from which I would experience solitude and quiet, acceptance from close friends. I needed to gain a perspective from which I could restore myself, minute by minute, day by day. I would grow in spirit and strength. The darkest of times would be accompanied by silver linings to strengthen my resolve to survive and thrive.

It took more than solitude and quiet to center and focus my path, though those things helped set a tone for my recovery. It took a clear and defining moment to change my path on this journey into light. A bright, young attorney that I found in the *Yellow Pages* – Joseph Tully from Los Angeles – kept me from going to jail for having not paying the required child support, procuring for me a favorable alternative of 700 hours of community service versus jail time. It took my oldest son Cedric, crying out for me to fight for him after an innocent chemistry experiment had gone bad, forming the basis for his living with me once again. It took my daughter Mia, demanding my presence regardless of what the court had to say about it!

Such incidents renew my essence of hope in all things possible. The journey from that moment on filled with community service, healing and serving others as well as deliberate promises to my son to fulfill his desire for freedom was a journey of never losing sight of the light at the end of the tunnel. I patiently confined my actions to things "of the tunnel" to maintain a clear direction, making all the difference.

And most of all, no matter the circumstance, whatever the obstacles, remember to count your blessings. Give tribute to those people who have affected us in significant ways; honor them in life and revere their passion and their passing. We know they are still here with us in spirit guiding our direction every step of the way. Jerry Thomas Murphy was such a fantastic person, larger than life, taken from us way before his time. Always screaming at me as we swirled upon the dance floor, "Isadora, don't go changing!" He took me to baseball games, dined with me the very first Thanksgiving I was alone, choosing to be with me rather than his family. We walked the Lafayette Reservoir, we danced and sang together until we cried. I often hear Jerry saying my name...Isadora everything will be fine!

nia, marry, have lots of babies and commence the building of our large happy "European" style family. On a rainy afternoon, July 1, 1987, we wed, surrounded by friends and family at the Old Country Farm Church. Flowers and design work courtesy of Filoli Flower and Design Shop, north of Greenwich, Connecticut. My mother assisted with catering for six additional elaborate weddings the same weekend in and out of New York City but one would never have known. Champagne was flowing for all. The guests were in awe. The cake driven up from Manhattan was a European Bee Hive.

Our picture perfect affair had many interesting underpinnings, though no one would know. The facade was like a performance perfected to flow from start to finish. I was raised to be a performer. The show must go on! Our wedding was followed by tours of the Metropolitan Museum of Art in New York City followed by a honeymoon to Bermuda and an elaborate trip through Europe and another ceremony in Portofino. Together, we traveled and experienced a wealth of adventures. I felt the love we shared for each other and I wanted so much for our budding relationship to be perfect. His strong desire to own and to control me was overwhelming.

I did not conceive the depths to which marriage would change my life to one dictated by someone who had to have things his way. His demand for total control was in large part cultural; however there must have been demons lurking.

Years went by. The good memories I have – that day in the solarium, for example – come with no pictures of Oberto. He simply wasn't there. He found his life best connected to the "Club" and his people. He found little pleasure in spending time with us; our small children were my task. I was not as he "expected" I should be. I sought out the company of au pairs to care for our children and make our home feel complete. The emotional estrangement between my husband and I turned violent as Oberto became more controlling, displeased by his inability to change me. I became his irritant. He demanded power and control and in all ways. I was forbidden to enter "his" kitchen.

One night over one altercation I became fearful for my safety and that of my four small children. The police saw the effects of our altercation. Oberto was taken away in a police car. The next morning he was returned to our estate crying and sobbing for mercy, saying he would never ever do anything to upset our home again. He was not dumb. Quickly to suit the needs of the audience of viewers, Oberto learned his lessons well, hiding his rage from all to see. To others he appeared cavalier, the perfect husband. In the quiet of our room, I would become the outlet for rage, suffering immobilizing panic attacks which left me curled in bed where I thought he would inflict the final blow. I recall kneeling down to kiss his feet, begging him not to explode in front of our precious small children.

No logic or words of wisdom worked against his demand for total control and conquest. Regardless of all my attempts, "Woman is to be ruled by her man." I was repeatedly threatened about my insubordinate ways. I was told if I so much as tried to divorce him this was unworthy behavior of a wife. If I left, I was told the house would be burned to the ground with all of us in it.

Erratic behavior and threats of violence had me constantly escaping with my children to the coast. My family did not understand my moods and anxiety. No one understood my desire to take other jobs and or numerous projects to stay busy and out of his way all of the time.

Though I could have chosen to stay at our estate, I sought ways to get away mentally and physically with my children and with the au pair to a variety of destinations – Maine, Carmel, Palm Springs, Los Angeles, Caribbean Islands, and Hawaii. I applied to school, believing it would provide me self-affirmation to keep going strong within the relationship. I tended to drop any and all charges. What else could I do or become? If it was possible, I would do it to keep us together.

Sex was fabulous with Oberto. In bed I allowed him to take charge, submitting totally to his strong toned body. I closed my eyes and dreamt all was perfect in our reality; that there was nothing but my imagination that was leading me astray. I created a picture perfect masterpiece and vowed to face yet another day committed by marriage and our four adorable children. Although each climax was exceptionally brilliant, one miscarriage followed another; stress seemed to control my actions, hostility was coupled with verbal and physical abuse and further isolation from myself and my sense of security. I was totally overjoyed when each of my four angelic children were born (all natural births as Oberto feared medication). I would forget for a moment our immense differences reaffirming our commitment to the long term! Family was a force that bound us together. I had to strive to have more children and be the best mother despite his ways. I had to survive.

Despite my attempt to forget what our reality was and to

be "perfect" in his eyes, I was not perfect. His temper would rise up and command the stage, yet again accentuating our differences. I was not a "mother" as he expected I should be. Everything I did or said was the beginning of a start of another confrontation so I chose not to speak around him. I felt trapped, preferring passiveness to outbursts though it seemed I was systematically and routinely attacked verbally and physically in front of my children. I defended myself by screaming back. I saw the panic in the eyes of small children. I admit to one abortion. There had to be a finale to all of this.

I filed for divorce with a brilliant young attorney who had offices in San Jose, California and who seemed to have the interests of my children and my safety at heart. She saw abuse and called it. My ex investigated this person, which was quite extraordinary as I had never informed him of my inquiry. He showed up at her office one day, perhaps following me in my footsteps, demanding she stop ruining our marriage. When papers were served, I called her office to drop charges. She was horrified by my lack of follow-through. I suppose as I had been coached throughout the night, I was more fearful of leaving than of the prospect of staying. Horrible turn of events. Oberto promised he would never again have a violent outburst. He did not let up. In disbelief my attorney consented to my withdrawal of a demand to be heard about episodes of harassment and violent outbursts. In the eyes of my attorney, I was undoing my only chance at justice. She was right. Though a charge of abuse would likely have been a successful tactic resulting in full custody of my four children, I was unable to bring myself to imprison the father of my children. Justice would have been served. I blocked my own chance of freedom and justice by allowing fear to rule.

Violent outbursts continued despite assurances otherwise. I felt broken. Oberto offered demands for me to change, to become "better." I was threatened, pinched, told I was insubordinate and imperfect. The "me" as I knew it was filled with imperfections, recounted in detail in front of my four impressionable children. In exasperation he would attempt to rattle me by twisting my arm behind my body to get me to listen to his logic, my memory forgetting minute details of each incident as a safety mechanism to my soul. I was pinched so hard I would bleed and bruise but I had come to the point I would not flinch and I would try as best I could to ignore.

Babysitters asked about the bruising covering my arms and legs. To seek to minimize the questions and the incidents, I slept in my son's room in his top bunk. I developed a skin condition which covered my arms and hands with sores requiring me to be bandaged from exposure to scratching. I developed an anxiety induced wheeze with asthma symptoms. My health in jeopardy, I orchestrated a plan to secretly escape with all four children, to get away and reflect upon our situation, to heal and perhaps submit paperwork for irreconcilable differences.

Oberto knew my plan somehow. He alerted the local police who immediately decided to descend upon our home and take our children back to their father. It was thought I had "stolen" children. I was seen to be the one endangering gentle young lives, taking small infants and small children from their beds. In actuality, our move was to create safety for us all. But my desire was undone by my lack of confidence and follow through. When I presented my essential factual evidence to the judge all the evidence I had to present was overruled; my facts never considered. Oberto brought to court a powerful attorney claiming I had run away taking my children into hiding. "Argue the facts, ma'am."

When the die had been cast, Oberto was chosen to be the sole physical custodian. He repeatedly threatened me to stop interfering with his parenting. He warned neighbors about me. The kids were his property; I was not to be involved.

He called the police frequently, making repeated reports about my insubordination. I displayed to Oberto irrational attempts to see my four children. I was told to simply go away. Out of desperation, I signed over my portion to our gracious estate believing he would soften his stance and allow me to see and be more a part of my children's lives. I incredulously believed giving up the home and all of my possessions within the home, I would be treated more fairly. Not only was this not the case, I was garnished child support and further taken to court for a charge of contempt upon the court for not paying sufficient amounts.

Oddly, the court seemed to me to caress his ego, making his story and ego more secure. He acted and played the part of the perfect parent. He was a stronger person in that he carefully followed all the rules as dictated by the court where as I was never one to live by rules or constraint. Every demand by the court seemed to work to his advantage. His control and domineering mannerism urging me on to make one change or another was my undoing as I often acted as "putty" in his hands. I would make moves he would anticipate and call the police accordingly. Oberto was systematically getting his revenge. There was no fair game playing here.

Our long, drawn-out divorce was finalized in 2005. Physical custody of my three sons and one daughter was granted 100% to my ex-husband. In large part to testimony of a private evaluator who, at best, saw me as a laid-off professional who dreamt of becoming an attorney, capable of earning significant money as a nurse. The judge agreed with her assessment of me and ordered me to pay large sums to my ex. I had little evidence of stability – no furniture (left in our estate with Oberto). Oberto had disallowed me possession of a family car. Judgment rendered by professionals who believed what was in the best interest of all our children.

*Focus*, I was told by each attorney I consulted to reverse custody. *Focus*, they would say to provide for a stronger retainer ($40,000 up front). "You need to focus." Hindsight is better, of course, than what we have to work with at any given time under the heat of the moment. I am not a fighter type. I was not a fan of divorce, nor what divorce stands for. This was a battle not made for children.

I had every intention of staying with my husband, of having and raising a large family; the goal was to be happy. It seemed to me that the commitment to love and to cherish was breached from our inability to compromise on the differences between two people from vastly different cultures. Oberto lashed out when I refused to mold my behavior to that which would please him. I became afraid of what Oberto was capable of doing to further to disrupt our existence. After episode after episode of bullying and uncontrollable rage for which I was the chosen candidate, I didn't love myself, which affected my ability to fight hard to win. Enormous focus was required to have my children back. I was stunned by the process.

There was no way to explain the feeling of disbelief to have a judge say you are no longer custodian parent four times over. I had small infant and toddler children. I was the mother of these children. I naively imagined the presentation of volumes of factual evidence, filled with emotion and passion for my sons, would be sufficient on the face of it. I had come to court feeling self-righteous, determined, privileged. My fear had been the unknown of demanding to divorce someone who came from a culture where women did not step outside their boundaries, they do not divorce. I told the court how I deserved the children; what my ex-husband had done to uproot our precious family.

The attorney for my ex had a quick and brilliant response to everything. "Objection, Your Honor." All my evidence was found to be "procedurally incorrect," none of my evidence was taken into consideration.

Clear and substantial factual evidence with no emotional upheaval must be presented in custody dispute cases. My evidence was not allowed in. Furthermore, I had dropped charges against my ex-husband for numerous important factual and substantial incidents of abusive behavior. The credibility of my story was now horribly tainted. I loved my sons and my daughter immensely but I was scared to death and was not focused in the war I was waging against someone with a strong constitution to win. How could I ensure the safety of my children if

I was unable to fight the battle? The judge and evaluator sided with my ex-husband.

Oberto remained in the Saratoga house, a stronghold interest. Going forward, I was told I had to provide evidence to the court of a "substantial change in circumstance." Their assessment of me was final. I was found inadequate to be custodian parent for four children ages from six months to four years.

From a place of loss, I forced myself to stay in flow and be positive with and for my children as if there had been no judgment. I was in disbelief that someone or something other than the mother could make decisions to take my children from me. Boldly, I was going to go against rules that sought to restrict my access. I would find a way to nurture my children regardless of my limitations as my life depended on this giving of love and support.

To strategically ease myself into a position more likely to allow me more time with my children, I became Oberto's babysitter, providing babysitting service for free while he attended evening law school. This expanded my allotted time of only two evenings each week. This was all good.

I attempted to gain custody of my four children on a variety of occasions. On each attempt I was either denied a forum or all credible evidence was objected to and the motion was sustained. At one point, Judge Libby demanded I refrain from making further "futile" demands upon his courtroom. Nothing I had done would cause a court to take one baby, let alone four babies from their mother. Persuasive arguments aside, I did not drink, did not do drugs, nor did I live an extravagant lifestyle. The facts: four young impressionable children were denied a mother by a system which excluded the whole truth.

Pediatricians banned my ex from their offices due to the out of control rage reactions observed during his visits to their offices. Numerous neighbors expressed concerns for the welfare of my daughter and our three sons. Despite friends and colleagues saying not to worry as I would definitely get my children back, key facts raised by neighbors and physicians were denied significance by key decision makers.

One perceptive CPS counselor promised to return the children to me stating she "could not believe our outcome," vowing to reopen an investigation. The inquiry went so far I truthfully believed I would actually gain back custody. I was in tears thinking someone else finally saw the truth and called it. Then came an unexpected phone call: "We are so very sorry. The decision to return the children to you has been halted and overturned." No clarity was provided during this escapade.

Despite the air of privacy surrounding my case and the hidden facts that needed to be aired in public, those facts were not aired. My family was baffled by the untoward turn of events. I chose to be silent going forward as it was easier and less painful than continually sharing my sorry story. I enjoyed moments with my angels the best I could; taking them on mini adventures – to Carmel by the Sea, to Capitola on the beach despite having to return them to their father each and every night. It became part of who we were and how we managed our lives to enjoy the moment. My focus remained always on the children. I recall days in fall, the leaves would blow all around; very special times holding hands rollerblading. We were filled with magic and laughter! Mia once freed of roller blades would dance about!

Once back to my cozy warm apartment, exhausted, we gathered in my large bed watching Fievel the Mouse in *An American Tail*. We squeezed tightly together all of us in my one big bed. I was perfectly okay during those times; the experience was comforting and delightful. I took strength from each experience and vowed to make the next experience even better. I pulled away from the judgmental contact with my family (sadly) who demanded to know why and how I had been denied custody. What had I done to deserve this? I hid from peering socialite friends. I could not cope with judgment and I knew they were talking.

Work became my solace, nurturing others, especially babies. Going forward, there had to be acceptance of what was, tempered with good humor and an effort to be at peace with a situation that I could not immediately change. I could not financially come up with all what was demanded of me: "substantial change in circumstance" The weight of the punishment, I was garnished to pay my ex. I had already signed over our house. My need for an abundance of material possessions and trips and travel which had formed the basis of my upbringing diminished. The comfort and presence of my four children filled me.

The local country church with its warm and welcoming parish took me into their community with open arms, looking out for me, allowing me to pray openly for some kind of peace and stability amidst the storm. I prayed again and again for the safety of my children while this amazing place provided me large rations of bread, some money in times of need to support rent, a sense of belonging which I had long since forgotten was possible. Easter Sunday, 2005, I joined this congregation. This place of worship and non-judgmental people gave me a sense of peace and resolve to accept what was and to share love and compassion with others. I prayed openly for my children, we verbalized concerns, we had celebrations of peace.

I picked up my children daily at the end of their school day. They liked where I had come to live; the warehouse and the farm surrounding this oasis, calling it "Mommy's farm." They watched cows grazing in the distance. Mr. Rasmussen, the owner and oldest cattle rancher in our area, would ride down the hill in his tractor. He was big and tough, with an enormous smile on his face. He wore a cowboy hat and authentic cowboy boots. All three sons got a big kick out of Mr. Rasmussen and jumped and danced about his feet. Mia adored the horse he rode upon. There were no harsh words. There was always kindness. We selected fresh vegetables from the fruit stand, cooking them in a steamer. All experiences we did together in survival mode, simple, lighthearted and filled with joy. We came to laugh often!

I got used to the warehouse and the farm. After a bit of white paint, second-hand carpet, linoleum floor, and redecoration, it was cozy, light and airy. Outside, with the windows open and the breeze gently blowing, the farm was vivid green, tall green willow trees surrounded by rolling hills, a variety of fruit trees and horses grazing. A large bountiful organic garden with rows and rows of herbs, select varieties of colorful summer and winter vegetables including pumpkins and wild flowers. The sustainability of natural beauty reminded me of an Italian villa. Years later, I would recreate this peaceful oasis-like surrounding at a farm I call my own.

I offered to pay for this sacred place after my initial free stay concluded; the request was denied by the owners. This wakeup call was an unwelcome change as the warehouse had become a sanctuary. But I remain to this day grateful for the time and experience and expressed this genuinely to the owner. It is not every day someone offers a room up for free to someone in need. This person understood the value of giving graciously. This stranger was an angel.

The place I moved to was close to my children, close to the library, and allowed for us to spend quality time together. Soon after this move, the landlord made numerous unwelcome advances that I refused. He subsequently refused to allow my children entrance to his home. The stay at that house was short. It was again time to move on. My children were my primary responsibility.

The demand to create the "substantial change in circumstance" permeated my spirit. I had obtained a real estate license in Baltimore. A friend Christopher urged me to take classes to sit for the California Real Estate examination. By day, I studied essentials of real estate while at night, I worked as a nurse in Atherton. I passed the real estate exam and would come to sell homes in Woodside.

As a staff nurse, I had benefits, consistent money coming in, and a solid base of support from friends who acted the part of family. Now, I could show the court stability and change for the better. I was offered greater management responsibility as risk management analyst. My self-confidence grew and so did my ability to network and see tangible growth for me and my four children.

When I moved to our first one bedroom apartment I was beginning to feel I could actually make it! For the first four months, Catholic Charities paid our rent. Much of our money went to feed growing attorney expenses and counseling appointments for each child. We ate at a Sizzler Restaurant with a supply of coupons given to me by friends and co-workers. Afternoons, we enjoyed the quiet of the public library. Otherwise there was always running, soccer, and rollerblading. Mia preferred ballet and theater.

From my ex-husband's perspective, I was his babysitter. He would tell others, "I do everything for these children, they are mine." I was required to live by his rules or else. Occasionally, my four would be dragged screaming away from my presence while grabbing hold of my legs and my arms. Oberto blamed me for these episodes, as if I caused them. Again and again, he would summon the police to call attention to and report I was blocking custody rules. Moreover, each time made the police more upset with me than with Oberto. Though I tried to take attention from those horrific moments, they were what they were: outcries from all of us out of control. Sadly, I acknowledged my children were coached to be drawn away from me. To the benefit of my four children, each one of them in their own way continued to love and look forward to our times together, never once rebelling against our visitations.

There was nothing to fill the void and emptiness that such isolation breeds. Though I saw my children more than the limited segments of time I was to have been allotted by the courts, it was never enough. I grieved at each and every one of our transfers. I cried in silence. "The children are my possessions," Oberto would remind me. "Stop blocking me from taking my children." It was extremely difficult to maintain composure and control of my emotional state. I did not want to further upset them, yet here were my babies being dragged from me and crying out!

More years passed. Each child has grown older and wiser than I ever was. Every day I adored each one of them more. Each one is more beautiful than the day before. Interestingly, each one looks out for the other in a solemn pact dictated by honesty and trust for each other. They have an uncanny ability to sort through all they had heard, and love simply and completely. They adapt to whatever their environment, I suppose in order to survive having been carried from one place to another. They had no choice in this matter.

I spent the next few years trying to tread water, never succumbing to the currents, determined not to drown. I chased coattails of men believing someone or something would save me or teach me some special solution that would at once absolve us from this predicament to allow the formation of that all important "substantial change in circumstance" the court so wanted of me. I obtained knowledge; I was determined to develop our base of support.

I committed to continually enrich myself with knowledge and expertise. I gained professional certifications to enrich my path and nurture my children to greatness in pursuit of their greatest passions. I sought always to create the "substantial change" in the midst of chaos that would allow us to be as one. Real estate transactions came and went, stock market investing profited and then fell. Insurance, philanthropy, and nursing allowed me to give freely of myself. All passions became intertwined as one. The course clear. The bottom line: I was on course with my children to survive and to thrive.

Select entrepreneurial investor "boyfriends" influenced my life and my lifestyle to bring me all the way back to the risk taking and feeling of ability to do and be all I would want to be from the past. Selectively, each "boyfriend" came to offer advice and encouragement. I allowed them in because of their brains and abilities. I enjoyed the benefit of communication, of companionship, selective interchanges when convenient, immensely elegant restaurants, theater productions, musicals, and moments of sheer delight and passion. Still, I would remain focused on my children. My present did not allow for the creation of a future with another.

My son Cedric continued to send me emails when we were not together describing our "family" home; Oberto had come to deflect his domineering and controlling nature upon my eldest since I was no longer there leading to Cedric feeling caged. Cedric detailed verbal as well as physical abuse directed at him in ways that were different from normal teen defiance of adult authority. I encouraged emails so that I would be able to support my son 24/7. Ongoing communication was essential for both of us as of course I feared the worst. Though I never admitted to my fear for his safety, I wanted my son to know I was always there to listen to him and to provide a consistent forum for him to vent and release. I recall one time I went to pick up the children to find Cedric disheveled, curled in a corner of his room. Despite all our time on the phone, it was not nearly enough time to ensure my son's safety.

Domination and rage against me had been consistently overlooked by courts. I would never ever allow the threat of, and actual, harm to my children to be overlooked. Cedric described being told by his father that I was evil and not to be trusted. Cedric was told his father was in control and that his father owned and ruled everything. Cedric was being forced how to think and made to act. I listened intently to this gentle beautiful impressionable son and feared for his safety. I also feared for the safety of my other children. Though strong in my constitution, I was constrained in action by a court that had the power to judge me as inadequate and imperfect. Cedric's communication with me was a cry for help.

As a result of severe and constant control placed upon him in often out of control ways, Cedric acted out. Though Cedric remained a straight-A student, he hung with the wrong crowd. He dressed in only black, became less verbal, forgot to bathe, and went so far as to say he felt "caged." When I found him curled in a ball on the floor of his room, my concern shifted to alarm. Not long after, school officials reported Cedric had performed a chemistry experiment at home and had brought it to the school. The act on school grounds was forbidden; he was to be punished and expelled per protocol. The root cause went beyond a momentary experiment; a troubled boy sharing an experiment with classmates was not to be tolerated period. To the world, this boy would be punished for his actions. Oberto wanted no blame shifted upon himself for the act of his son. The custodial parent forced Cedric to move out. I saw a hurting boy, immediately placing my protective wings around him.

I listened to my son. I did not think about the act nor its consequences. I immediately moved Cedric into my apartment, removing him from all atmosphere of doubt and ridicule, relinquishing my bedroom to make it special and uniquely his own. I gave all of my effort thereafter to nurture and heal a troubled son who just months earlier had come to me expressing feelings of being caged by someone who sought to control with rage reactions. I sought the expertise of counselors and clergy, enrolling my one son in an upper level school close to my apartment. I vowed to honor my one son unconditionally as I would do each and every of my other children. I vowed to shower him with unconditional love, trust, and a feeling of being wanted. The new school enrolled my son in all upper level AP classes. The principal welcomed him with open arms. My son joined the track team.

I sought the expertise of Adam Kennedy, a top family law attorney who had worked with me earlier in our attempt to get custody of my children. I came to him now with the intent to file *In Pro Per* ("by one's self") to act as our own attorney. Mr. Kennedy, Esq., believed we had sufficient evidence "if sustained" to go to court on Cedric's behalf to file a motion for a change in custody and to be successful. My son expressed his steadfast determination and commitment to succeed in this process to get out from under the confines of my ex-husband's house. Cedric was now of the age to provide his own testimony. I gave one-hundred percent to this effort. Many a day I sat preparing the Motion for Consideration. I recall more than anything the feeling this brought, "Mom, you must fight harder, we must win"!

Something here had changed. We were not trying to win, we were going to win. From Cedric, we had to win. We lost on our first attempt because we were denied the right to have my son testify; the presentation of oral evidence on his behalf was needed if we were going to be successful. Despite our loss, we were again encouraged to file yet another motion; a Motion for Reconsideration. The time limit to prepare and submit the reconsideration was ten days. After lengthy deliberations, my son was granted the right to testify. There were no restrictions ordered. Judge Porsche in the past had consistently ruled in Oberto's favor.

Debra Solland, a legal advocate, encouraged us to handle all legal documentation professionally and pro-actively. I did exactly as she advised providing ample copies, sending each package directly to the judge on time, in advance, cleanly, neatly, and well organized. With the courtroom cleared, but for lawyers and my ex-husband, Cedric spoke slowly and confidently answering questions I posed.

In clear tones filled with honesty and conviction, my son was brilliant, presenting his truth in front of all to see and hear, never faltering, always maintaining eye contact with our judge. He was dressed impeccably. He testified to ongoing verbal and physical abuse and acts of rage; he detailed being physically marked and feeling caged in thought and act. He expressed an unequivocal desire to move out of his father's home, he wanted a future without conflict in an environment where he could be respected and where he could thrive. It was amazing really, listening to Cedric, who just months earlier, I found curled in a corner, battered and empty. From love can arise a freedom to transform oneself.

Cedric demanded of me to "fight harder." We succeeded in having all essential testimony considered for our carefully crafted and deliberately prepared Motion for Reconsideration. As a result, judgment was rendered in favor of my son. I recall the day Cedric swirled me round and round my one bedroom condominium apartment after opening the envelope to receive the result we had waited so long to hear: he won! The aura of the moment filling us both with happiness, freedom, exhilaration, and excitement. Our fight for justice came with amazing rewards. We no longer were forced to hide, free to embrace and "be" with each other without limitation. All things are possible to those willing to never stop believing. A great victory won by those doggedly determined to persevere.

Valuable lessons dealing with lawyers and judges and ex-husbands. In one day immense life lessons; my precious young child taught me the patience and perseverance to win over doubt. The world can be inhospitable at times, a place of violence, a place of cold and blatant injustice. It is just as easily remade by those fearless and able to speak the truth. Like most things, it all starts from within. Cedric affected change that day and for that, he is ultimately the healthy one!

# CHAPTER TWO

# The Power of Positive Energy, Tunnel Vision Style

*Saving one individual at a time from the effects of violence, trauma, and abuse is the paramount objective. The "Tunnel Vision" methodology is simple to implement yet profound in how consistent implementation and follow-through will positively affect outcomes in each life it touches. The goal to save children and adults from violence will be achieved for all who embrace "Tunnel Vision"*

**W**hat I developed as a by-product of my journey out of the depths of despair and back into a world of promise and beauty was a process I came to call "The Tunnel Vision Approach." It was a shift that would crystallize my path of focus and clarity of thought. I created the approach for me alone. I came to see this methodology as something to share with others.

Though the Tunnel Vision approach is confining and narrow in focus, it will allow for the simplification of life, leaving behind the fears of the past to allow for an awakening of the soul. I visualized an architecturally perfect tunnel spectacular in every way. I visualized light and peace; a simple framework to work wonders to empower me as my own inner architect. From a position of pain, I had stayed wallowing there for oh too long. I began to crystallize my thinking, create an imaginary safety net shielding out noise and distraction of a harsh and insensitive world. Suffice to say, it worked for me.

The Tunnel Vision approach takes a hurting individual bound to the past to a place of peace and quiet. It allows in no manipulation and violence. The world is filled with distraction. To awaken the inner spirit, one must get beyond distractions however it works best by creating a roadmap or simple directed course of action. No one other than you has to be aware of this master plan. The goal is to nurture healing; to recover fully body, mind, and spirit. Energy must be directed always to self-growth, self-discovery, and self-love. Life is a gift; not meant to be destroyed.

A commitment to change must be clear. There are ways to successfully cushion lives surrounded by brutality. There are ways to speak, to act, and to focus to promote positive energy flow and to enjoy a healthier and less troubled fulfilling post-trauma life. A learned behavior pattern of focus on one's passion and one's being is utilized to reduce the likelihood of the perpetuation of trauma. Self-empowerment is brought about by consistent nurturing and loving support, backed by disciplined imagination and focus, will lead to a more stable and violence-free life. For my children, designer- dancer, artist-golfer, sax man-musician, and analytical chemist-winemaker, all of their chosen passions are brought to light.

I have experienced success from a process of unwavering commitment to self-actualization, enlightenment, and patience. To be alive in the moment, not look ahead too far, and certainly not look back. We cannot recreate the past events. The past is what it is, injuries nurtured, the soul gently healed and fortified. It's okay to take comfort in what we have been through, yet to experience today in all its glory, we must not stay in the past. We must awaken to love the moment, and allow things to be to be set free. There are ways to awaken from within. One must dare to dream big and imagine all possibilities. *Carpe Diem.*

Judgment is excluded and acceptance provided with open arms. To calm the effects of trauma, love and support must be unconditional. To avoid the erosion of self-worth, positive energy must be always present allowing one to open slowly petal by petal. If one sees self-destructive activities, we deal with them immediately in the open without judgment or fault. Gentle strategies are utilized to guide one to self-acceptance. We nurture others to heal with love and tenderness of spirit.

In the case of Cedric, I began to nurture him with consistent care, consideration, and acceptance tempered with much time off to eat much and laugh often. It took time for him to open up but every pizza was worth it and every drive in the small black beetle bug to the Santa Cruz coastline to learn to drive a stick shift was worth it. Some of the best conversations occurred in the long sessions going from first to third and back again until we mastered the steps with confidence. It was here, I saw the power of my simple methodology to help others to heal.

A commitment to focus on the good is summoned and reconfirmed on a daily basis. For it is within the "tunnel" of our own making that we focus and choose to free ourselves from patterns of negativity, terror, and pain to create a place uninhibited to allow ourselves to dream and soar. From total despair, miracles happen if you believe them heart and soul. I am graced and honored by my eldest son, Cedric, who demanded change as he had come to a place of sufficient self-love to demand care and concern from others. From a place tattered and beaten-down, my son emerged with lightness of heart. From one point where my others sons said "why help Cedric" emerged a miracle. "Mom, I am no longer a caged animal."

Cedric is now a top aspiring chemical engineer, a winemaker, and intuitive. He has grown to be confident within himself; he shares love easily with others. He has evolved completely and utterly from a core of self love. What we did together and what he worked on in a spiritual way worked magic which will last him lifetimes. Mai graces me with her warm and dancer like spirit in her passion and alignment with design and fashion. Alessio provides me with wisdom, demonstrating the importance of listening and not speaking. He has chosen to put an end to any incidence of trauma by acting the quiet and always centered philosopher; a certain candidate to become a pro golfer if this be the road he wishes for most. Zubin is filled with art, music, and theater; he lives to embrace the moment, fluidly and openly challenging himself to achieve personal greatness, aligning himself with the audience, his music comes alive!

Healing is a happy process. In time, flow just happens. You no longer having to remind yourself to maintain focus; it guides your path unconditionally. For me, there was a specific day when I instructed myself that this "was it." There was no turning back. I felt this moment and announced it to the universe! I was okay; as I walked on, I was guided by my inner compass. It has been my self-imposed contest and challenge to do more, to be more, to accomplish things I had only before dreamed of. The vision and focus to trust in all things possible!

Create an architectural rendition of a picture perfect life.

# CHAPTER THREE

# Passion

*Continued patterns of violence, harassment, and abuse eat at the soul and psyche of a child and destroy the capacity for passion, courage, and self love. Effects of abuse may be clear immediately or effects may wait till much later to emerge. Cries for help and acting out in maladaptive patterns may be seen by professionals without prior exposure as truant, unacceptable behaviors. We may inadvertently punish a child when in fact the cause and effect of damage was initiated by a violent and abusive parent or other party.*

Clear, unobstructed passion for your own success and that of others will provide a disciplined focus to allow dreams to become your reality. I imagined success with a total commitment to what it takes to achieve this goal. I think of this in great detail always surrounding myself with images and positive affirmations to make this real. I press onward without looking back or questioning whether I am capable of this to the extent of my quest.

The practice of passion is a disciplined process. This path has me focused on outcomes to affirm truth and clarity of purpose. During the past two years, nine strikes have come to disrupt the calm of caring for infants and mothers. To stay within my comfort zone, I acknowledge the hospital is what has saved me, to simply be allowed to "nurse," to nurture others freely and completely, to feel the affirmation of genuine trust and caring. I found in nursing others a freedom from oppression.

Where before I imagined confrontation making me guarded with each interaction between my husband and me, we have come full circle to a place where we strive to practice non-violent communication, a movement away from fear to the centering of spirit and being. We exclude patterns from the past that would lead to trauma and abuse for the benefit of our children. We are conscious of energy flow, on our walk, how we contemplate goals, how we engage ourselves with others.

Trauma experienced by victims of violence is overwhelming. There are insufficient coping mechanisms to aid healing as manpower is required. For those attempting to survive, patience is our kindest gesture to return others to a point of healing and self-acceptance; the process must be individualized. Exercise your right to speak your peace. Assist others through the process. Sadly, all will not be healed as immobility is the easiest route. Breakthroughs are wonderful when accomplished!

Pain perpetuates pain. Oh how I lived and breathed it. People treat those in pain differently than they treat others.

Thoughts that we have been victimized hold us back and our energy reveals our stance. Pain and discomfort is simply where we are or have been. It takes on an energy all its own. For me, internal pain expressed itself in my aching back despite the fact I am quite active and limber. I reach forward to achieve an acceptable "close"of this manuscript. A strangely familiar pain grabs me; a spasm reminds me to stay true to myself, focused on what is important in this lifetime. I do care, to love completely things that keep passion in focus.

Remember to gently adorn yourself with grace and dignity throughout the many phases of your life. Proceed with pride, stand straight and tall, speak with promise and confidence as words you speak express themselves in the outward manifestation of actions taken. Hang to the coattails of others but be aware of the fact we are all imperfect. Having lost all sense of direction and being told I was not worthy took its toll. I lacked personal focus and creativity which took me from my true course of action, I lost valuable time I will never have back again, time away from loving my children, time away from centering on my core growth. Perhaps this was to have been an essential part of the learning process. I have risen above the past now, you must do this too!

In the end, triumph over tribulation is the most powerful teacher. I have seen the bottom and for a time, you stay there, somehow feeling safe and secure, crying out in pain, blaming others for your grave and sorrowful condition. But you come to see the time and attention it takes to stay affixed, giving to others every movement that is your own. If you delay growth, fear becomes who you are and how you are defined; it becomes a message you send out to the world, to anyone with whom you come in contact. Time is required to tell your story, but then change is essential, life is in constant forward motion and clearly this is the wave of the future.

Acknowledge personal suffering and afterward, it is time to move on.

As for Cedric, he started from a place curled in a corner in his room. Soon afterward, he saw nothing other than personal victory for self and for his team. He had come far in not accepting a feeling of "being caged." He screamed out forcefully demanding change, clear and directed in pursuit of a goal to become a top research chemist. Cedric evolved with love and nurturing, a process magical to embrace.

CHAPTER FOUR

# A Commitment to Change

*We think, read, and study stories of others. Each story is important, all words have credibility. We advocate for a system of justice, where substantiated facts, however emotional, are embraced, any and all documentation is memorialized, violence is minimized and ownership of children and adults as a form of abuse and manipulation is eliminated.*

Over New Year's dinner in 2008 at Bistro Giovanni Restaurant in Carmel, California, we laughed, enjoying the moment. We went around the table of dear close friends sharing our most wonderful thoughts and dreams for the New Year! I made a commitment to myself and shared this with those around me, envisioning the sparkles and shining of a New Year's Eve. Filled with hope, surrounded by my dear select friends, I said would have a country house; I would get back my children!

My friends were smiling and ostensibly supportive. I'm

not sure any of them believed I would move forward and end up accomplishing what I did. For me, there was no turning back once the goal had been verbalized; it was time to seize the day! A total commitment to "tunnel vision" must be summoned and reconfirmed on a daily basis. A process of self-actualization, enlightened visualization, and total commitment must be reaffirmed verbally and then substantiated in writing on a daily basis. One creates a perfectly designed tunnel, focusing on it and moving forward to attain one's chosen pathway. I love the outdoors, therefore I imagine an arched pathway; I nurture this pathway with water and fertilizer until the way is transformed with brilliant green grass. I am protected, therefore I move along confidently and expectantly inside this imaginary tunnel growing roses here and olives there, always thinking of new and delightful possibilities. A trust totally grounded in the belief in all good; I am willing and able to dedicate time, attention, and a commitment to the journey; a focus of body, mind and spirit where no doubt or negativity invades this place. A commitment to healthy living will further nurture the processes.

A progression unfolds naturally as baby steps are taken and dreams are accomplished. Words, actions, and one's spiritual being are in clear and unwavering positive alignment, accentuated by dance, rollerblading, swimming, and passionate living. Movement was central to my times with my children either competitively on the soccer field or together running or bicycling to the farmer's market. Lightness of spirit aided in creating our magical times together allowing no stagnant energy in. One becomes a vehicle for affirmative movement in one's ability to change with grace, peace, and dignity. All of us moved together in unison, we were one.

You put down the violin, stop playing the overwhelming story of doubt saga and move ahead gracefully to places filled with hope, promise, and exciting new tomorrows. New and alive stories do not involve words about a painful past. It's an awakening of your special creative genius – an awakening filled with joy and happiness. To create all possibilities, free from the past, one must speak joyfully and embrace the moment. For the lives of my children, I was committed to change. Though it took time and patience, I did move forward for them and with them.

The scenario in retrospect: I dropped charges of abuse again and again out of fear of the unknown, desperately wanting to maintain a picture perfect image of family. I had four beautiful and perfect children I adored dearly. I had an executive level job with promise and opportunity but was recently let go because my boss was retiring. I had bruises covering my arms and legs as a result of our altercations. Oberto, meanwhile, was sitting on our couch, a laid off gorgeous Italian picture perfect executive, depressed, self absorbed, shouting out orders and reading philosophy books. I kept the au pair around to maintain a sense of happiness versus gloom and doom.

I encouraged Oberto to move from the couch, to become engaged, to seek new things, to attend law school. He was bright and his future was promising. He had moved to this country to accept this one job. I bought a bicycle for him to go riding with me. I smiled and worked two or more jobs while the au pair watched the children. It had to work!

Perhaps his sense of self was affected by his job loss and the woman (me) who did not subordinate to his every demand. He directed his rage and attention on my imperfections to maintain his sense of control and his dwindling self worth. Though I wanted to be present at all times with my precious children I wanted to run and hide from his often wild and out of control attacks of my character and abilities. Abusive episodes mounted in private and in front of our small children until I began to suffer physical symptoms – asthma and skin-related conditions. Oberto would repeatedly threaten. "If you try to leave, I will burn the house down." I had to be okay. I had made a vow to stay married for life. Often I cried in silence.

Attacks on my psyche and my body were revealing. Others began to question the presence of bruises and my uncharacteristic trembling. I took the advice of an attorney from a help line service, not knowing where to turn. She did not intimately know our story; the advice was free. To find a safe place of hiding until I could obtain a court date to discuss our issues. Buying into this plan, I stole away away in the middle of the night with all four of my children plus the au pair to a quaint cottage house on the coast. It was an unoccupied old farm house with views of the water. I knew the sellers could not sell quickly as there were major structural problems with a bridge and foundation. I managed to create an agreement with the agent and the owner to stay as a renter with reduced rent until the house was sold. I imagined healing from rage to start fresh, to rebuild our lives.

Oberto found out about my plan. I suppose he went through my purse and found enough evidence to alert the police. The same night we arrived the police were summoned to bring all four of my little ones back to Oberto. When I questioned the logic of taking four small children back to an abusive man who they knew had a history of violence, the police said either we all go back or they were taking the children back to their home, period. I was in shock.

Oberto informed me we would keep things simple with low expenses. Behind this veil of secrecy, he would not allow divorce, he would not allow a win. He sought in every way possible to make me appear the bad guy, make me look as though I had abandoned our home and our family. He would paint a horrible picture and share this to alert others to my "evil" ways. None of the truth as I saw it was included as evidence. *Objection, Your Honor.* "Sustained." No evidence of violence and no evidence of danger to the children were allowed to be revealed. Oberto quickly took on the role of the perfect father in front of the court. He learned also how to tell all others I must be punished for running away with "his" children. As a result, judgment rendered by the court, Oberto got the house, the boys, and child support. I became outcast despite all my friends saying "truth will be revealed".

Faced with an unimaginable reality that was court ordered I was in shock. There was nothing that would separate me from my children. I could not accept the fate handed to me as I could not embrace a body of law telling me I was inadequate as a mother. Oberto seemed to weave his magic and withhold the truth so as to win. He wanted control more than he wanted to love our children. He had to win and he worked this win with strong and persuasive arguments within the court. It did work

A court is not always the proper chamber to dictate where a child is best loved and adored. If facts are not portrayed accurately and honestly by the proper professional advocates a court will not see clear where a child is best protected. No amount of money paid to an attorney to win a battle in court for custody and for control will weave the best outcome for the child's welfare. Here, a grave injustice was committed when my children were allowed to be placed in harm's way.

I stayed "put down" by order of the court, an uncharacteristic role for me, for a very short time. I would have to live contrary to the court plan of action as nothing could keep me away from my children. No issue of judgment telling me I was not the custodial parent could change the character or quality of my life. I would see my children whenever I could and however I could. Oberto took my attempts to be with my children as opportunities to place me in a bad light. The police were frustrated, Oberto wanting to charge me with interference with custody orders. "I own these children." I would continue to pick up the children as no one else was available. I would continue to care for the children as I was their mother. Essential evidence was barred which would have illustrated grave concerns about the safety and security of my children. I was made to be the outcast. Oberto made it clear: I was no longer the custodial parent.

"Mom, fight. Mom, you are not fighting hard enough." These are the most powerful words a mother can be gifted from a child. Clearly, it was my son who catapulted me onward. Though I am positive and forward looking by nature it was the few words by Cedric to move me in ways that chilled me to the core. I could no longer be emotionally driven. Going forward, I crystallized a vision with total commitment and passion, conscious of perseverance without fear and without looking back. My steps were constantly controlled and contained. Attempts at tearful interludes of "poor me" were met with blind eyes and empty glances. I was committed to personal self discovery and self growth. I was committed for the sake of four amazing children to be strong for them and to create clear substantial change.

I demanded freedom from hostility, violence, and control; however I failed to get essential factual evidence in front of the judge. Our judge embraced "arguments" made by the opposing counsel because of their ability to present and carry the day convincingly. Judgment rendered; where does one go from here? Emotional outpouring of passion does not make a case. I was denied access to four small children whom I loved dearly. I saw it as my right and light of my life to see and be with each of them daily to read and to hug. I was judged to be in contempt of court by not paying sufficient child support, a move made by Oberto to further incapacitate me. I was ordered to go to jail. Was this all a bad dream?

Even from the depths of despair, I began my recovery process, gentle and nurturing to teach self love and self preservation. I believed in my heart and in my mind my children loved and needed me. I believed in myself.

One must pause; before we are able to move on, we must

have a healthy appreciation for our own well-being and satisfy our own needs and desires. As I, you must exercise your right to speak your peace in order to move forward to make miracles. Breathe deeply; baby steps are possible. Thoughts that we have been victimized hold us back. Become the heroine. I turned to the volumes of journals of my childhood; my outlet from years ago during times of high anxiety to create poetry, verse and rhyme. I created lifetimes of happiness within one page and then another. I dreamt of moonbeams. I would begin again to write and dream.

Body awareness including stretch and dance kept me fit mentally and physically. I would spend two to three hours a day in the gym doing cardio exercises followed by a full ballet bar routine. I would turn the music loud and dance with abandon. A spiritual awakening occurred when I exercised for long periods. Emotion would overcome me; yoga, to ballet to core strength training followed by rollerblading to evening dancing! From a time of painful remorse I remained fit sufficiently to breed a healthy mind. One's energy level reveals one's stance. Rise up and lift your head in grace and pride. Stand straight and tall and speak with promise and confidence. If you feel obstruction or pain, recognize this and work to remove the blocks that bind you whether in mind, body, and spirit. Dare to find truth always even if no one else can see what you see. Never move from your intuitive core; trust in your power and strength to drive all action positively. If you find yourself lacking energy and clarity, sleep more, nurture self, rest the mind, seek calming images – a place, scenery, beauty. Plant a tree, sing verse to enlighten your path! Share this if you feel inspired, smile, touch a child. Remember to breathe!

Observe the olive tree as it bends gracefully with the wind, flowing and rising up to stand straight and tall. Allow yourself to rise up and face each new day with promise. This morning, I examined all two-hundred-plus olive trees that grace my farm. Last winter was bitingly cold; numerous days of frost and low temperatures. One would have thought all my trees would have been lost. I gave each one a name, spoke gently to it, touched it and imagined it growing and flourishing. This morning I arose to see a small branch breaking out of the earth! Life flourishes when nurtured.

When Oberto returned to work and began law school as I had encouraged, he needed a consistent reliable babysitter. I became that for him. It was difficult having to say goodnight to each of my precious little ones at the end of the night. I wanted to put my babies to bed and read them story after story. I was blessed to have found a night nursing job which allowed for the parenting schedule we now embraced. Oberto appeared now more stable, non-violent, as he calmly went about his business and seemed to have learned his lesson from my alerting the authorities to his violent tendencies. He continued to tell others I was not the custodial parent.

Eventually our divorce was finalized. The children expressed their desire to not be moved from house to house in the middle of the night. From the court's perspective, this moving was okay and nothing was done to affect change. I did see subtle problems and took action pro-actively to keep in tune with the effects of our hostile divorce. Alessio stopped learning the alphabet and was regressing in thought and actions, withdrawn. This was reported to me and I began to volunteer in his kindergarten class. I could not be restricted from this act. I emptied my retirement account to take him to a specialized school designed to work with auditory and visual deficit disorders – Lindamood Bell Learning Systems, a program for children with learning disabilities, some originating due to specific stress trauma.

Alessio and I attended sessions on a daily basis for a couple of months. We built lasting memories as Alessio worked with a man named Pat. I remember holding Alessio's little hand as we walked in the rain in downtown Saratoga to get a steaming hot chocolate. These sessions worked magic on his confidence and abilities. Alessio was transformed by these sessions.

Cedric seemed to be more and more fearful of joining groups, showing behavioral patterns that warranted concern from my perspective. He would cringe and hide in the corner when I took him to sports. He would say, "Mommy can't you just come back and live with me please?" I would tell him, no my wonderful little prince, mommy cannot do this. Together we would cry and hug tightly each other.

Mia became more and more demanding when we were together, exhibiting temper tantrums that in the end exhausted the both of us. I enrolled her in ballet, jazz, and acrobatics to create an outlet for all the energy and emotion inside that needed to be expressed in a productive manner. Zubin, my young star seemed to escape all harm. Oh, I loved my children so!

I cannot forgive a system for a decision to allow custody

to be given exclusively to Oberto formerly found to have violated our safety. No one but me seemed to see problems brewing inside our four small children. I am not certain what possessed me to sign over our million-dollar house other than to ensure my children's safety. Perhaps I believed Oberto would soften. Perhaps I believed, as I had always been taught in Connecticut, I was invincible. Perhaps I thought I would be saved by someone or something. Oberto did not outwardly say he would abscond with the children to Italy, however this thought was always in my mind as a definite possibility. He declared, and the court affirmed, that I made excellent money. It was decided I should be the one to pay child support. It was absurd, but it was granted. I was not working full time but the court set child support based on a nurse's full time salary. I found it impossible to pay the person who had taken my children away and declared me not fit as a custodial parent.

More devastation: Oberto informed our judge I was not responsible. I was charged with contempt of court on eleven counts for not paying sufficient amounts of child support for all four children. On Friday morning the judge informed me I would begin jail time. Could I begin immediately? I told the judge I had a responsibility to pick up my children after school and this outcome was therefore impossible. I was to report back to court on Monday morning for sentencing.

Shocked, scared to death, I appeared again Monday morning with attorney Joseph Tully. I stood there trembling, knowing I could not have taken one second in a jail cell, let alone six months or more. Joseph methodically convinced our judge I was not a criminal but a mother. Joseph pleaded my sentence down to seven-hundred hours of community service.

Afraid of what would come next, I had to keep moving forward. I now had a responsibility to the court to give back all seven hundred hours, actually a blessing. With time limit imposed I was determined to act fast. In the hands of any other attorney, I would have been thrown away in a jail cell. Joseph Tully argued my case and reasoned with this judge to my benefit. This was the first time the judge had sought to see reason to benefit our side. Bravo Joseph! I did volunteer training for CASA (Court Appointed Special Advocates for Children). I became a docent at the local museum and I provided neonatal resuscitation education to physicians in China. All activities enriched me in many ways.

I remained free to love and nurture my four children. I signed them up for soccer, football, piano lessons, swimming, tennis, and dance. We traveled to many fine places around the bay area; the Legion of Honor, the Exploratorium, and Carmel. I bought each of the children roller blades.

Law school for Oberto was a huge commitment of time and energy. I was his constant and loyal babysitter. This time of babysitting became my parenting time. I honored my boys and delighted in their presence. I began to feel I could make it, if I could just make one small improvement in myself to benefit my children each day.

I didn't know it as "Tunnel Vision" at the time, but part of the ultimate commitment to moving forward was a tight and narrow path required to heal my soul. It became an active plan with no room for doubt and no turning back. Positive affirmations and self-love to constantly nurture spirit, I created a unique vision for me alone, a tunnel of sorts. I committed to work at this master plan every minute of each day, becoming more and more self-assured, until I succeeded in my goals. I lived the plan, morning, noon, and night. I came to love myself completely, keep my own counsel, being at one and totally accountable for my own success. I did not depend upon another to create or mold miracles. This is not easy, but this was ultimately essential to succeed. We must paint a perfect picture; make it your reality!

Should you choose to succeed, be determined to count your blessings each and every day, write about them, journal them. Energy must consistently be directed to those actions consistent with your tunnel vision ideals. There will be moments of paralysis, fear and immobility. Perhaps we pause to have a chocolate or two, go for a run, join a friend for a glass of wine! Feel the immobility, breathe into it, do not stop feeling exactly what you are feeling. Perhaps write about it and somehow make it your friend. Allow this time to be a quiet experience. Provide yourself with the time and tranquility to feel, to always feel, to answer personal questions, and to speak to yourself with gentle guidance and love. It is okay to be human and to not be perfect. Recognize limitations, then call to action the movement of mountains.

Experience each moment; feel it, live through it day by day. Draw upon the experience and grow to accept what you have gone through. Reveal yourself to others. Laugh about your limitations. What we say matters, how we think and what we do, even the smallest of things. The effects of your words and your actions will follow you always. Know your boundaries. Watch patiently for breakthroughs!

The time in the warehouse had expired and I was "encouraged" to move on. I joined St. Gregory's Church, to stay focused in prayer, acknowledging aloud we would find our way. Catholic Charities provided financial support to rent a one bedroom apartment, a step in the right direction. I filled my days with exercise and babysitting my adorable children, returning them to their father late in the evening. Self-healing came from loving my children, dance, ballet, and healthy eating. I was warned by the police and the courts about breaking rules and not fulfilling "a substantial change in circumstance." I cautiously progressed step by step with all eyes watching my steps. The church provided bread Saturday mornings.

I began a night nursing job. I became a California real estate agent. Miracles happen. We would survive, taking baby steps one after another with my children as my greatest advocates. Silver Linings are everywhere.

# CHAPTER FIVE

# A Spontaneous Life

*We provide for health care professionals a "stepping-stone"
methodology called "Tunnel Vision" to assist in the development
of a sophisticated Plan of Action. A disciplined plan builds focus
and clarity to aid in healing an affected child and family in emergent need of support as they move from a troubled cycle of violence
and reactive mentality into a pattern of healing. It is crucial for
the child within a troubled family unit, affected by drama and
harassment, to maintain a sense of self, stability and spontaneity
while going through traumatic scenarios. "Tunnel Vision" will
assist in establishing mentally and "for real" a forward flow away
from effects of abuse and violence. The urgency of this plan cannot
be overemphasized. The time for action is Now.*

All material items I had come to surround myself with
became his items; he signed the backs of professional photographs, books, all things material. I embrace the past despite
its upheaval. I did away with material groundings. I maintained

a vivid imagination, loved to be and dream creatively. What mattered: my children.

Children's Hospital served the basis from which I nurtured babies during the night. Caring for others completed me. The hospital is where I found a home: friends, families, and babies in need of nurturing. It was amazing giving to others, leaving work feeling totally fulfilled. It was fabulous.

I met Isaac at the farmer's market. My sons and I had just returned from a trip to Kennebunkport, Maine to see my family. I was running and my children were bicycling with glee through the farmers market stalls. Isaac stopped us and encouraged us to taste "the best nectarines." He found us again on the other side of the market and shared with us amazing whole grain breads. He invited us to his home to see his flowers he purchased at the market that day. Isaac was a doctor. His house was filled with flowers, fine art work and books. With him, my life would become spontaneous, carefree, and interesting. Everything was a possibility. He was a man who loved life, loved people, shared passion for life by vacationing and dining out, music and adventure. He proceeded as though each day was his last. It became a whirlwind, everything an adventure, hard not to grab hold and run with it. I felt alive and compelled by Isaac's energy and spirit of freedom. He bought me clothing and took me to the theater.

I thought I could not be replaced, obtaining a massage license to ensure I was indispensable. I lost weight to fit into the perfect Victoria's Secret underwear. I wanted to be for him the perfect nurturer. Magical time with Isaac took away the loneliness when I was not with my children. It clearly showed me that there was another side to life that had nothing to do with struggling. He taught me about travel, he taught me about business and investments. He exclaimed, I was perfect and did not hold me up to scorn. This period of time was good for me. I knew Isaac loved variety in life and that included other women. Often he would wander.

Isaac encouraged me to learn about the stock market. The markets were another one of his passions. Together we performed stock trades during a hot and often volatile market. I got a job working for Paine Webber. We created a learning environment within our relationship based on the markets while I sat for and obtained all of my essential securities licenses. At the outset my career was over the top. It was commonplace during the height of the bull market to see stock portfolios appreciate twenty to fifty percent annually with trading of new technology stocks. I was successful making Isaac's portfolio grow though mixing business with pleasure was something I was advised to avoid. I had not listened. Isaac encouraged me to purchase a condominium for my children. The condo was beautiful. Another goal achieved. I did it! A perfectly wonderful investment it was.

My life with Isaac was completely separate and surreal. I didn't want my children to take information back to their father, information that could be used against me. Rarely if ever would I share times with Isaac with my children. So there was football, soccer, piano, dinners together– time spent with the children in the evenings. There was also time for counselors for Cedric and the others. I would then be invited to go to Isaac's house and have a whole other life filled with candlelit adventures and nights walking and talking about life. We fit naturally together for a time – passionately, spiritually, and intellectually.

Oberto, jealous of my change of fate, pleaded for me to come back to him. He confronted Isaac at the Farmer's Market, saying how much he loved me. Isaac disliked this confrontation and took issue with being what he saw as harassed. I did not blame him for he did not ask for this and Oberto was his natural and controlling self. I remained focused on nurturing my children first and foremost. Though Isaac supported me and my dream for healing and peace grounded in a belief in miracles, I acknowledged that time with him would come to an end.

No matter how much I tried doing "all the jobs," Isaac left me. Notwithstanding our hard-earned Certified Market Technician titles, we both lost hard in the fall of the markets during the technology crash and it would cost us a relationship. I was the easy target; I had been warned first to not mix business with pleasure. We ended as quickly as we had begun.

Oberto warned me that this would happen. The stark change in my day to day life gave me a renewed focus on the issues that now surrounded my life and my children's lives. Oberto and I came together mentally at this point; we both saw damage mounting in all of our children, especially Cedric, due to our high conflict divorce. We collaborated going forward in the concerns we had for our children. I would not have believed from the wars of the past – the courts and child protective services we could become so healthy. We had mentally and spiritually come far.

Though the relationship with Isaac failed, I enjoyed our

times and what the relationship symbolized about life and commitment to loving another. Page turned, I was ready to return full throttle to the task at hand of being ever present for my children. This would take everything and then some. But it was time.

I thank Isaac for his love; for never questioning who I was. Every moment was lived as if it was our last, fully and with excitement and joy for every meal, every theatre event and every song we heard. I did not look back from this adventure, we danced everywhere we could and whenever we could.

There is a time for all things; that time in particular was filled with self-exploration and self-expression. Isaac symbolized life and love in all its glory. I welcomed love in, danced, played, believed in angels and miracles. It all awakened in me a deeper love for self, love for others, a steadfast loyalty to others, being with another as never before; no rationalizations.

# CHAPTER SIX

# Expect Silver Linings

*We provide creative ways for the individual affected by abuse and trauma to put an end to the "puddles of pity." It involves a decision to love self and want for healing enough to make a decision to throw away the emotional violin, and move forward positively. From painful and destructive experiences, we share the tragic harm that violence and trauma has, long-term, on the isolated child and family unit. We share the discipline, patience and creativity necessary to change a negative and destructive pattern of activity into a positive forward moving pattern of establishing goals and dreams. Without this "forward flow" and without careful and consistent intervention, children and adults may become injured psychologically and immobilized physically for the long-term, causing irreversible pain and destruction to the individual and the family unit.*

I successfully molded a process of movement based on needs and the requirements of my children. Instead of giving an incident tragic significance, I gave it power, energy, focus; nurturing attributes toward a positive end. I did not look back – even once – to those who would have questioned my actions. I did not listen to anyone who would influence me in a negative fashion. I moved onward, nurturing my four children. There was no choice; I had to secure freedom from violence.

Isaac gone, I was free to focus on my children who needed me most. Oberto came to me, pleading with me to move back into the estate home. Perhaps he felt Cedric's pain and realized then that things were beyond his control. He even offered me ownership. I refused. I was dealing with a lawsuit with Isaac.

In the midst of all chaos, Marella Bloomberg sat across the table from me. My attention in life had been diverted to Isaac and his needs. "I came to help you organize," she said. "But you must do some of this yourself." I recall the pact we made that day to change our lives for the better for both of us. She transcended magically and quite astonishingly, going on to attend S.F. Art Academy, Parsons School of Design and would not stop there!

I was in a good place. I had my condo and my night nursing job. I was back on my feet, strong and thriving. Everything was going to be okay. I could breathe and enjoy for a moment. This was about the time I received a call from the high school. Cedric had created a science experiment and had brought it to school to show off. No one was injured. I was asked to come quickly, to be there with and for my son. Was everything okay? We were in fear all along that something like this would take place. We are brought to realize the seriousness of our journey and how what we do affects the paths of others. Cedric was seriously hurt and affected by our trouble.

Close your eyes and paint a perfect masterpiece. We who accomplish much in this fast-paced society should remind ourselves daily to breathe, to enjoy and find laughter in the simple things. Spice and charm in life enrich the spirit and keep you young. In truth, we can create the spice and richness of spirit from within if we allow this to be so. I often wonder why I could not simply go outside our estate and nurture the grounds. It took time for me to learn the skill of quiet enjoyment of the moment.

Vow to keep a journal of your thoughts and expressions. Encourage written imaginings to fill pages with your dreams and expectations. When I receive a note from one of my children who is sharing a special thought and feeling, I embrace the magic of thought transformed to paper as the greatest of personal gifts. All the colors of the rainbow scattered about make a collage of magic to light my day! I would live for one more sentence and one more passage and one more scribble! Thoughts and hand painted masterpieces expressed on paper are miracles. "Mom, thank you for being the best mom ever, I do not know what I would do without you".

I arrived at the hospital to be informed I was not on the schedule. As I turned to leave, there was a call summoning me quickly. My son shared a homemade chemistry experiment with friends on school campus. Thankfully, to the relief of all of us, there were no injuries. The act was done quite innocently, however there was work to be done in unraveling the reasons why. An explanation was in order from my son, a chemistry honor student. The school requested my presence.

All at once, a quiet, withdrawn boy whom I had recently found curled in the corner of his bedroom disheveled and unkempt was front and center. We were surrounded by FBI and the bomb squad, not to mention CBS Channel 2, all of whom descended upon the school campus. There was no one to ask whether the boy had frequently been curled in a corner, "owned" by someone who was trying to get even with me. Expert analysis rendered: my son had conducted a chemistry experiment not involving explosives which had been brought to campus quite innocently but not allowed just the same. This presentation of such an experiment had led to a stir on campus of a magnitude significant enough to scare people.

Oberto was in shock; he literally threw Cedric away, writing a note and signing it: Cedric had to move from his estate immediately. This act was poised to distance father from son so as not to be perceived at fault. Oberto would allow the courts and the school to do as they pleased to be seen on the side of the law. He did not want to be connected with the promoting of such activities. He clearly and unequivocally abandoned his son and his best defense. A Silver Lining occurred in the midst of the storm created by an unwavering need for my presence. Oberto's attorney, "This boy will most likely be punished."

In an isolated moment, an immense feeling awakened me, beyond the self-absorbed doubt which had consumed me for so very long about my role as custodial mother. A critical moment for me to travel beyond tight court imposed limitations. I snapped into action, acting quite beyond the parameters as set to restrict me, hiring Joseph Tully, the same attorney who successfully represented me in my contempt of court action. Something in my son made Tully realize we were dealing with a damaged and hurt child; we were not dealing with a criminal. Cedric was a chemistry wiz, period. Again, the best of evidence had to be revealed.

Joseph Tully presented successfully to our judge, with great finesse and confident speaking, and in the end winning the case on behalf of my son. There was a presentation of honor awards in chemistry and physics. There was the publication of science articles. There was a declaration made by Cedric apologizing for his curiosity and inappropriate display of chemistry experimentation on school campus. Caution to the wind tempered with knowledge, we all must be cautious and careful when science is involved.

My son Cedric, in turn, saw the depth of my love, caring and respect for him. We came very far, doing simple things from the beginning we had not been able to do from all that time being taken away every night. He was in the process of learning to drive a car. We would take the beetle bug to the Coastal Cemetery. We would drive until he mastered my clutch. All the time in the world could not replace those special moments with my son on those occasions. We both came to know each other again. We also ate a lot of pizza somewhere along the way.

I grew to feel wonder and embrace the moment every day whatever the consequence. I continued to listen to joyous music, to jump, and to dance. Say "I love you" to your children and mean it! Give an encouraging comment to a young adult. Smile and make someone's day. The commitment to growth one baby step at a time is mandatory – to smile is life-giving. To share love with another – so long as it's tempered with a kind and gentle spirit and a remembrance of the personal things: a kind word, a caring touch. Reach out, make a difference, love and embrace someone with passion. Surprise someone with a miracle that lights up both of your lives with sparkles and sunshine. The giving doesn't have to be returned.

It is in the giving that we are made whole. Empower yourself daily with words and actions that you are a superior and phenomenal being, worthy of being successful without abuse, trauma, and violence. Every person, irrespective of age, has a story waiting to be told. Allow this time, and then move on with grace and clarity. For the moment is now. All we have is this time to express our dreams and empower our miracles.

Pray at this moment, heal away the pain. Never say never again. Miracles are everywhere, make them happen and you will awaken a spirit inside yourself. You will become an example of peace and tranquility. Mia and my sons saw the troubled road Cedric was heading down. They often would say, Mom, why fight for Cedric? He should be punished. I knew what they could not ever have known. Cedric was raised by a scared and angry man whose sole objective was to create destruction in his path. Perhaps the road traveled by Oberto was paved with troubled stones and goblins. My son needed someone to nurture him, someone to cherish, stand by, and support him, period. There was no one there for him during these times. The system failed him greatly. This was my opportunity to love freely.

There was no choice but to take hold and fight. With this

realization, this amazing opportunity clothed in doubt from others around us, something inside of me changed in a profound and powerful way. Energy I previously scattered, aimlessly, non-focused, suddenly came together to compel my journey straight and clear. I was strong now and focused; there would be no giving up. We fight for our family, I told my three other children. We stand up for what is right for each other. To stand tall together when the chips are down were my greatest moments. I am proud of what we were able to do. Cedric is an amazing son and I love him dearly.

I recall feeling elation when the mail came; we opened the certified letter. I had been awarded sole physical custody of Cedric who had forcefully testified before the court. My son picked me up as we read the verdict. He twirled me around the room again and again. I remember his energy, his passion and his joy which filled the room that moment. He had won his freedom, he had been listened to. This moment was his victory.

Find happiness from all Silver Linings offered in this one amazing lifetime. The stimulation of our five senses: touch, taste, feel, hearing, and sight, should be embraced each and every day as we look forward with anticipation rather than looking backward. Learn something each and every day. Love someone and touch the soul of someone you care for. The love you give to another will come back to you tenfold. It is amazing what good energy can do once it is put out there for all to see and to touch. Dare to celebrate existence openly rather than to be fearful in life. Be a bit crazy if you must; continue always to encourage a vivid imagination, for with it we can climb mountains wherever we are and cross the widest of streams.

Create a burning desire affixed in your mind and go for it. Like a river, allow constant flow in motion, unabated, and allow the current to move you. We may feel we desire for things to move a certain way and therefore create the energy to set out to make change happen. Despite our efforts, we learn that flow is directed by nature, not force. Do not invest energy, time, and passion trying to interrupt natural flow. Allow what is; be accepting of life in all of its glory.

"Mom, work harder, you are not fighting hard enough." It was those simple, forceful words of a troubled loving boy coming through clearly and definitively that set my focus clear. There would be no turning back now. I had a powerful job and mission to accomplish, no longer immobilized by fear, pain and other such stagnant moments. Cedric and I perceived this situation as our last opportunity to take hold of my son, to work to create a common good for all of us; a silver lining with benefits whereupon I could be present to care and nurture this special boy. We were successful – a defining moment for my son and me whereupon justice was served.

I ask that you continue to see Silver Linings in everything that happens in your life. You are the chosen one for a mission of greatness. Give in generous ways so much so that you get back immense satisfaction from the experience of giving. Spread joy and it will be returned to you during your lifetime and afterward. Create legacies so as to memorialize and make more of one simple life – your own.

Make your children the masters of this journey and you will have been provided a vehicle for greatness. We share in tunnel vision, a driving focus to encapsulate your energy and thought processes to find a singular purpose greater than all of the pain you have suffered. Give the methodology of healing away!

I am not an advocate of an approach that mentors punishing children who act out by tossing them on the street, denying them love and respect. I seek out the downtrodden among us and give them a voice. All good is possible in all people. See this to be so. I came to experience, share love, speak with respect, and commit to spend one more moment eating pizza with my son, helping him learn to drive a stick shift VW bug through the cemetery. Small talk and more small talk. Time is the better medicine. It takes time. Spend the time!

We came to share constructive ways to nurture children and families who have suffered the effects of abuse, trauma, and violence and move on to succeed in harmony with others. Nurture your spirit with child-like intensity each and every day.

# CHAPTER SEVEN

# Commit to Know Thyself

*Creative intervention must precede financial and emotional destruction. We caution those individuals involved in crisis mode to employ "more thought, less emotion, before action." We advocate for more creativity toward a pattern of "Tunnel Vision" to direct forward positive action. The court advocates for 'Substantial Change in Circumstance" in the midst of the most emotional of circumstances. To "win" and to be healthy, a consistent focus on health and healing will fuel a more peaceful and profitable outcome for all! Overall, one must have love for self before anything is possible. "Be of love, much more careful than anything." Teaching love and self respect is the key to healing.*

Commitment to the Tunnel Vision process demands of one to look deep within one's own psyche and historical background and upbringing, even the upbringing of one's own parents, retracing patterns of the family's past to see why or on what basis violence and harm is tolerated. It requires thinking openly, not being afraid to discover and know truths, perhaps hidden ones. For history repeats itself.

My mother's parents emigrated from Ireland. My mother directly competed against her parents by opening a flower shop in Greenwich. She was always strong and independent, a Martha Stewart type, a designer and businessperson. She took her work seriously – no alcohol and lots of coffee. She traveled to New York City and Boston from Greenwich early in the morning, collecting flowers, decorating bar mitzvahs, weddings and funerals. She was successful as designer extraordinaire.

My dad's family was of German descent. He was more a people-person, a greeter type, the Kiwanis guy. Mom clearly overpowered him, but he loved her just the same. The two stayed together to make certain we grew up safe and secure as family. It was clear they did this selflessly. When I went to Skidmore, the two separated.

My upbringing was outwardly fabulous, with skiing trips to Colorado, vacations in Maine, and summers in Bermuda. No expense was spared ever. As a young girl, I modeled routinely in the city, commercials and small things. I would understudy for the "Sound of Music" with Mary Martin. I danced ballet in a company which had the makings of the Bolshoi. Ballet became my life, my passion, molding me from the time I was five to sixteen. In high school I would do other sports, joined the ski team and performed in drama and color guard.

As for the presence of conflict in our family, I did not see or hear of it. My mother yelled often at my brother; I remember punching a hole in the wall, trying, in frustration, to get her to stop yelling at him. Otherwise my parents were too busy with a thriving business or perhaps I just did not pay attention. Looking back now, I can see that her temperament in those days was very much like what I would witness with Oberto. No matter what, I had my beloved ballet.

We are influenced by the actions or inactions of those around us. Inner strength of character allows us to grow despite distraction and destructive influences. Therefore, each individual must quietly make a pact with him or herself, to continue on – Tunnel Vision style – to achieve personal greatness – spectacular, self-fulfilling, self-actualized, impassioned greatness. We can achieve this if we put our faith in self and move on to accomplish our chosen passion.

Being a dancer kept me away from the noise and kept me in sync; a kind of "Tunnel Vision" way. One year I recall being told I would have the lead role in our company performance of "The Nutcracker." It was a very busy season for my mom. She was overwhelmed with her own troubles. Though I ran to share the news of my success, I was told there was to be no more ballet. If only I had been strong enough to find my way. I allowed my passion to be taken from me. Never ever do this.

Sadly, I felt my mother's pain; essentially forcing the marriage of my parents. If my mother felt she could not have happiness, happiness would be denied me as well. After being denied ballet, I began having severe panic attacks. I told my mom, I needed help, but her response was that I had to help myself. Luckily, my allergy doctor encouraged me to write about things I enjoy. "Focus on writing and your joys," he said. I began journaling, marking a sort of starting point to my journey.

Miracles are realized for those who listen to their own inner passion. Those who put forth an unwavering focus one baby step at a time will achieve greatness. The journey is simple, clear, and focused. Self actualization revealed!

At sixteen, I had fallen madly in love with a young man at our church group. Whenever our eyes would meet, I would crumble. Once, he came to our home to tell my mother how much he adored me. She told him to go away. We continued to see each other as if bound by cement in love. Once she went banging at his parents' front door to make me come home. I continued to see him regardless during college. Despite his proposal and my love, I allowed my mom's control and domination over my decisions. I never allowed myself to express my love for him fully.

When I left for Skidmore, my parents divorced though I would never understand the details. My dad gave her the house and the business and took some money and moved to Guam, then New Mexico. He never stopped loving my mom. I do recall there was no hostility in public. She began to date her accountant, then a broker, spending her nights in the city, going to plays and restaurants, hosting large wild parties in our home. At one such party she met an architect. Who can say what she saw in him? Though smart and artistic, excessive drinking turned him into a parasite. Down the road would come more problems with alcohol.

Some years later, the architect turned over the Thanksgiving dinner table when my brother Samuel reminded him that he was not our dad. The next year he would try to crawl into bed with me. Oberto, my future husband and father of my children, was a port in the storm, remaining cool and calm and worldly, when I needed his calming presence. Like the night at the expensive restaurant with the architect feeding my mother alcohol to the point of becoming uncharacteristically sick at the dinner table. Oberto was professional and calm not wavering, not judging, I liked that about him.

Before Oberto there was Valentino – older and not, of course, what I was "supposed" to be with per my mom. But we fell in love; in a single year we did more together than any other life experience, obtaining our real estate licenses and then some. I danced ballet with him and he encouraged it, buying bouquets of flowers for each performance. Valentino had a design shop. He embraced and loved me like a wonderful wild flower! But without my mother's blessing it would not work. Valentino intuitively saw bad times ahead for my family with the alcohol around and my mother saw a threat to her control and her state of intoxication. She forbade the marriage. I ran with Valentino to San Francisco. "Be of love much more careful than anything," he would say to me.

Oberto reminded me of my mom – an old-fashioned family man with a hint of passion. His power and need to control and be domineering were overwhelming. He said he was moving to Hong Kong for business. He said we had to marry now!

Make a pact with yourself to get strong and listen to your inner voice first. Do not hang on to the coattails of others believing another will save or complete you. For in the end, you will have completed or worked on other people's dreams and not those you set out to accomplish. Never place yourself second in line even if there seems some draw in another direction. Love yourself totally and most importantly, know who you are. You are the master of your ship; dedicate yourself to a forward path of growing one baby step at a time. Never look back in your quest for miracles.

With Tunnel Vision focus we embrace each moment. I spend my evenings creating gardens or creating writing passages. My mom lives close by; we have grown to love and respect each other. We spend our time walking her silver lab Liam, playing tennis, sailing, skiing, and enjoys her gardens. We enjoy moments shopping, traveling, and gourmet cooking. We do not look back to the past.

Be quiet, feel intensely, see clear and straight, acknowledge the truth in self and others, and move forward utilizing many, many baby steps. See how you hold your body, stretch in daily, breathe in good air and let go the bad. Know when your words are negatively focused and change them in order to reflect a kind and gentle heart. Shock yourself to change always for the better; allow positive change to embrace others. Love yourself unconditionally. Have the strength and commitment to move mountains. Chart your course of action to propel you onward. Let the tunnel vision I speak of comfort and guide you. Let go of the things you have no control over. The noise will be gone, the focus will become clear. Life will evolve as it should.

CHAPTER EIGHT

# The Power of Positive Energy

*Within jails and prisons, we imagine countless cases of in-jured misunderstood individuals whose injuries went unanswered, where inadequate intervention was provided within society. Perhaps those in society who cause the most destruction are, ironically, those who may have been injured the most. Once incarcerated, put away in cement cells, the treatment of choice: "no kindness or respect allowed." We nurture the negativity that has befallen the criminal. Gangs love and nurture violence. We are too late. Damage lasts.*

It's necessary to acknowledge that many will not be keen about what has come your way. In this sense, you may be on your own and therefore you must provide your own counsel and voice to move forward with confidence. Take peace and delight in the fact that you are aware of and know yourself bet-ter than anyone. Enjoy this fact and trust yourself completely. Always keep your eye fixed on the light and seek to love thy self completely, nurturing radiance and energy upon your being every moment of every day.

Create an image of where you would like the journey to begin and where it will lead you down the road. In your greatest imagination – the way you stand, the way you dress, how you speak and act – all become part of this voyage. Humility is key, for we already know and have encountered roadblocks that others would not even imagine could exist in one lifetime. We are never too secure nor too above it all to learn lessons along the way. Be open and accepting of change.

Quietly, with no one else around, call out your miracle. Make a promise to yourself that you will start on your journey and never allow your path to be interrupted. Renounce the past and vow to dedicate yourself to the creation of a perfect dream. Vividly imagine a perfectly constructed tunnel – beautiful, safe, and structurally superior. Become the greatest tunnel architect, going to any and all lengths to learn all you can and to command all the knowledge around you to protect yourself and, more, to flourish. From within your tunnel, moving forward, all things are possible.

Spend time learning a focused strategy. Surround yourself with the attributes of the tunnel – strength, focus, durability. The perfection and clarity of this image must be seen in vivid color. Understand that the tunnel will guide you onward. It is you, however, who must forge the path. What you do, how you act, and what you allow to guide you will influence the outcome. Let your vision explore the magic this experience will provide you. Make every part of the picture real in your mind and spirit. You are the master of your imagination.

Create for yourself a perfect environment in which to move past violence in all its shapes and sizes. Conquer and succeed. Verbalize the successes that will come your way from the framework of your master plan as though the successes are overcoming evil ways. As my one son Cedric described it in an entrance paper for college, "Sir Knight has conquered the dragon and succeeded in winning entrance into college." Win your own battles against that which is conspiring to stop you.

Commit to moving beyond trauma and abuse of all kinds. Vow to trust and love yourself completely. Stop dwelling on the pain of the past and turn away from the puddles of pity. Instead, surround yourself with healing and nurturing light. The past has enslaved and bound you, not allowing in the sun or a breath of fresh cleansing air. Allow it to enslave you no longer.

My children became my most wonderful blessings. Cedric, a fabulous, smart, warm, wonderful child. I recall delivering him and feeling as though my life felt complete. I walked from the delivery table down the hallway to my room. I felt amazing. I recall crying for days over how perfect I felt he was and how amazing it felt to be a mom.

Oberto from the start made remarks about how he didn't think I was producing enough milk, how I was not holding the child correctly. Instead of calm and consistent support, there were comments of inadequacies and imperfections. I continued to want to hold to the state of euphoria I was feeling. I came to want to have an au pair around all the time so I could drown out his words.

Alessio came very soon afterward. I recall he was induced

and was a more traumatic entry into the world. Oberto would not allow me to consider medications. I screamed and I do believe Alessio was stunned at the delivery. I encouraged them to check his breathing. The delivery stunned Oberto as well.

Zubin, tiny compared to the other two boys. He came exactly on my due date though at twenty nine weeks I experienced a high leak of amniotic fluid. Miraculously it healed over and I carried to term. When I entered the hospital Oberto made an excuse to go to a law class. I delivered Zubin quickly, with a tennis ball pressed hard against my spine. I recall one nurse, Karen, who never left the room. She was an angel. At the time, I was working as manager. I returned to work after two weeks of maternity leave. I avoided Oberto. My life was the boys.

And then of course there was my Mia. She came as my dream girl, pretty and pink. I believed all at once our lives would be saved by having a baby girl around to complete us. Quickly, it was apparent she was not only beautiful but smart and precocious. I was in love and quite content indeed.

The au pair too. I would have continued on but for Oberto's violent outbursts. Little did I know the path ahead would separate me from my children.

I came to believe that one should never give up the passion in this lifetime, never allow another to speak your truth. I tell this often to my children who are now all passionate beings. Hold firm to who you are, be capable of achieving all that you ask of yourself and more. Maintain a burning desire and a clear vision; create a positive flow of actions and thoughts. Allow for sparkles and shining light to appear.

Feel and believe you are just where you should be. Act with purposeful drive; be calm and focused on one thing. No matter how long it seems to take, feel the pleasure and joy that is in your path and embrace the movement.

Remove yourself from the noise and comments of others who are compelled to offer criticism and doubt. Allow only your vision to take hold and guide you forward. Stop talking, and simply feel this is so. Feel the truth and the light of your thoughts. Then move on and feel the reality of the vision you hold dear. Dreams and creativity will flow and miracles *will* happen. Fill your heart and soul with a realization that it is the perfect time to move on, and create your success story. The story of pain and sorrow will no longer fit for where you will be taking yourself.

Create in your mind a clear and vibrant picture of yourself in forward flow, moving gracefully through your tunnel. Once on track, there is no turning back. This process involves total commitment of body, mind, and soul; a burning desire for triumph. Picture in your mind *your* perfect peace, *your* perfect place to create. Go there often and dream. Reaffirm daily that this place is your reality. Voice this truth often. Once verbalized, it will be so.

Miraculously, the more you choose to direct energy on the path of healing, the more that healing will be achieved. Like-energy flows, so seek out like-energy. Flow with it. Continue onward, search for shelter and guidance within the tunnel. No one need know you are there. It is your own personal secret. One day, in the not too distant future, you will awaken; others will marvel at how far you have come in such a short amount of time. They will wonder how it happened. But do not get caught up in the emotion of their comments, or the extravagance of their praise. Continue onward. Do not stop your focus or commitment. The powerful flow of change will surround you and continue to guide you. This energy will be with you always. Whatever you vividly imagine with all your heart and desire with total urgency will surely come to pass.

Life was step-by-step after losing the boys. I never contemplated the possibility of staying at the bottom. I never turned to alcohol or drugs, things that would have taken me further down. The fitness center was where my body recuperated. The time I was able to spend with my sons – hanging at the library or rollerblading or bicycling to the farmers' market – was where I got my love and affection. The rest of my time was consumed with learning and doing – exploring life as massage therapist, esthetician, nurse, broker, real estate – to find the right mix and to suppress the thoughts of the past. Each day I found a way. Ask that your life be filled with golden opportunities. In the end, I was the master of my own ship, I had sailed through choppy seas, but I was committed to my journey with unwavering focus; it was my life. There would be no pain and pity from the past. There were mountains to climb.

Every day the mountains are in front of you and all around you. Choose to embrace them and make each challenge an opportunity. Seek strength from your obstacles. Climb inside your tunnel and know the direction and the destination from the first moment you begin. Be committed to your journey with unwavering focus. This is your life. There can be no pain and pity for the past.

Start now to embrace change. Close your eyes and dream. Take yourself away from all negativity and doubt. Take yourself away from those who would only wish to challenge your course. Always seek the highest ground. Love and be loved.

# CHAPTER NINE

# Love Yourself

*The juvenile court and the school system are visions of so-cietal violence. Such violence, caused by the early effects of abuse, neglect, and trauma must be eradicated or the individuals affected properly identified and cared for if we are to have a healthy society moving forward. Treating the effects of violence post-injury and post-abuse may be our only way of nurturing and healing. If this is all we have to give, we must give all. The approach of "Tunnel Vision" as a way to assist souls in need of a better way is far better than no intervention at all.*

I discovered that when one experiences the miracle of bringing a baby into the world, the most important thing to do is to continue to nurture yourself. A new mom, tired and exhausted, must draw strength from within, embracing the power and the glory of her own uniqueness, and from the miracle of having brought forth a wonderful new being. If the mom is disciplined enough to care for and love herself, she will establish boundaries for the success of her family. At any moment, we have the ability to provide our children with unconditional love and kindness if we have been healthy enough to care for self first. Rest and relax fully and completely. Set boundaries and care for yourself with all of your spirit and soul. Enjoy fully your uniqueness. Acknowledge your past and treasure your memories.

Try this: move to focus on the different varietals of the color green in plants and wildlife around you. As you expand your awareness, a virtual kaleidoscope of greens will come to you. Continue to learn and to grow with this thought. Each day, enrich yourself with a special gift you experience and cherish which is all your own. Decide to experience a small miracle every day. There is no cost attached to stopping to smell the roses. See the wonder in a small baby, a blossoming plant, olives on a vine.

Create a dream within your mind. Fashion the dream as your perfect and unique reality. Enhance the dream to the point of mental management and determination, seeing all the details and architectural designs to make it come alive. Fixate on the outcome you desire, as within a mental tunnel we continue.

Challenge yourself daily to touch, taste, feel, smell, and see life in a way that enriches you. Applaud each and every baby step you take. Reflect back in celebration and know how far you have come on this journey. Tomorrow, remember the little steps you have already taken and vow to go a bit further than before.

Stay young at heart and body. Be nimble with your mind.

Feel with your heart; jump and bounce and explore life. It may appear silly at first, but do it. This is all in preparation for the beginning of a life journey. Act as if you have just been born; act with an unquenchable curiosity for everything and no judgment for anything or anyone. Dare to explore life in ways not tainted by life clutter.

I have a dear friend Thaddeus; he jumps and smiles his way through life one day at a time. He creates and then recreates. I am comforted by his ability to make a play on life. He keeps all moments simple and at the same time elegant. There is no disorder to his thinking. I always feel him in the moment. Every breath he takes is full and fantastically beautiful. Every journey he experiences is meant to be healing and a joyous growth experience. This lovely friend does not look back nor does he spend time looking forward. He cares intensely about those around him. I am impassioned in the moment when I am around this man, for he creates surprise and intrigue at every turn. I feel honored in his presence. My son said to me the other day, "Mom, for some reason I am happy today and everyone I met was happy today." It is no coincidence that all energy of like quality gathers together and enjoys the union of positive flow.

Each of my neighbors embodies the spirit of peace and tranquility. Perhaps this is what drove them to move to this quiet place and work upon this sacred land. Benjamin walks daily around the vineyards with a huge smile upon his face. He embodies consistent and overwhelming joy on his journey. I feel this in his presence. The Aranda family delights in their ability to nurture horses who were previously neglected. They work the fields daily with passion, a simple task yet with the elegance of making the land a masterpiece. Upon this land now graze gorgeous horses who poise with elegance that is befitting them.

Olivier moved to this quiet valley long ago from Chile. He is pure Czechoslovakian by descent. He has come to own most of the grape orchards surrounding this quiet valley. He drives a red truck, his face is aglow, a picture of complete satisfaction. This land is his life. This man could teach us about miracles. The Liebherr Family is dedicated to the art of farming their land, tucked down a private country lane. One would never know the beauty that stretches out to encompass acres and acres of perfectly lined vegetables and fruit trees. They package, one-by-one, fully ripe organic melons to send to the local farmers market.

I join a reclusive writer as the latest new residents to claim an experience, to reach out and touch the earth. A family member and chef came to this farm from Australia to assist in farming, to experience where the fruits of his labor originate. All participants are impassioned players in their own life experience. There is dirt here, practically nothing else.

Miranda moved from Santa Barbara to embrace her love for horses. Emergency room physician Hugh commutes to emergency rooms around the West Coast. He designed a picturesque dressage and equestrian center to rival any I have seen from Sonoma to Saratoga. Wineries abound in the Appalachian region, creating "Best of the Best" of class. Dreamlike pursuits where dreams have become realities.

Make a conscious choice to dream big and successfully

live your vision. One does not need resources to dream. Pull from your dreams, call to your spirit to remember the wishes of your childhood. Decide when you are ready to take on these imaginings celebrating your uniqueness. Gone are the endless discussions of the past. Words like "try" and "might" are replaced with "will" and "just do it." Stop chatter and idle talk about things that were in the past. It takes time and attention away from moving forward. Watch what you say always.

Listen to those whose only path is to continually discuss the past. Pray quietly for them. Understand they most probably will continue to live in the past. I know this well; I was there. Pull yourself forward with gentle but firm direction in mind. Place yourself inside your tunnel, envision your movements every step of the way, move on, and pray for focus, clarity, and inner vision.

Allow yourself to love the moment with someone healthy enough to share it with you, not people who mentally are not present and accounted for. Not people who profess to be with you and are really with a dozen other people. It all goes back to loving yourself. Choose to surround yourself with like-minded people who understand your vision and story. You do not have to explain your actions or your vision. Do not apologize for what you are doing, you need no one to teach you this, it will simply happen. Time lost in blindly following the ambitions of others is a waste. This is time you could devote to chasing your own moonbeams. Miracles are there for those chosen few who have decided to follow this simple course of action. Everyone comes from a different background and mindset. Coping mechanisms are taught to us as children to assist us in getting through life. Those of us who experience trauma, violence, and pain will either move through life with grace or become frozen in time due to the inability to cope.

Some of us relearn more appropriate coping mechanisms by guiding and focusing ourselves into tunnels for protection, guidance, and precision of vision. This is okay. This works. Those around you may offer opinions on why your life is as it is, why the children are so, why you have lived deep within yourself.

Family members may state they know your pain, but clearly don't understand your actions. They may hold you in judgment for not writing, for not calling, or something they drum up as a reason to criticize and doubt. Understand, these are their opinions which you don't have to embrace. Be open to your growth and be gentle with your soul.

If you sense yourself feeling persecuted, stop blaming others for comments and judgments. Simply pray for those who may have wronged you. Take the focus back upon yourself and improve upon it day by day. Move at once from this energy-robbing process. The emotions of pain and victimization harm only one person – you. You have no time for idle wanderings of the mind. Step completely outside the environment in which you find yourself, create for yourself the strongest, thickest, and most efficient tunnel to shield out the noise, and create a safety net that is in harmony with life. This tunnel is yours to keep.

This tunnel which will discipline your vision and your movements will set you free in ways you will not see for a while. Keep the faith. State your intention to the wind and begin to march forward. There is no turning back now.

The emotion involved in loving and cherishing another soul is healing. Find a way to dedicate yourself to a project of giving back. Research those who are open and continuous in their giving. This is a mind-expanding experience. If you don't know about another, you may think this person to be other than how they come across.

I know a doctor who appears aloof, but secretly her efforts and life savings go to the building of a hospital in India. This doctor works miracles every day. She silently goes about her business, and then sends thousands of dollars to India, keeping almost nothing for herself.

Understand the workings of charitable organizations. Learn the benefit of charitable trusts and how they work to empower families. Build and nurture a commitment to future generations by giving back. A lifelong legacy of planning to benefit more than oneself is an enriching experience for everyone involved. I seek to become more knowledgeable in the area of charitable giving, with people who think big. I believe these organizations thrive and succeed as a direct result of their giving nature. Those who give get back tenfold.

Be a vehicle for change, vow to delay gratification and instead allow a work in progress for others. Establish a "medium of giving" to provide for self and family but equally as important, for others less fortunate. When we give graciously, we get back lifetimes. It is a karmic experience. What are you doing each and every day? Create a thought process that leaves you richer at the end of each day which is in actuality a step forward to a new beginning.

Embrace a legacy project now. Dedicate yourself to any and all change necessary to make this experience a reality. Should you need to read and enrich yourself further, start today to make this happen.

Planning and work is involved so take steps to learn, grow, and foster the experience within yourself and those around you. Should you need to strengthen the tunnel to allow for the focus and the clarity of thought, then do so. Make a difference each day and learn that in this moment there is no time to grieve longer than necessary. Become a part of the healing experience today and every day. Dedicate yourself to enriching your life and the lives of those around you.

Some who reach rock bottom allow themselves to be victimized, abused, and traumatized by the pain and sorrow. They allow the cycle to continue until it destroys the very core that binds them. Emptiness can take away the ability to act with intention. This state can leave one aimless and with the feeling that others will complete or enhance one's wholeness. And so we look outside of ourselves for someone or something to supplement who we are.

I lost four infant children, my career, and all of my material possessions. I became homeless as my inability to focus and grow consumed me. The extent of the experience of my pain became my existence. I continued to grieve for what seemed to be years. Time wasted, a spirit immobilized by immense loss. I probably would have gone on telling this story. It took my son crying out for me to stop and fight for him. This allowed for me a defining moment.

From the depths of my sanctuary – the place where I

ended up, a "warehouse," with no hot water or facilities – began my humbling experience. Years later, I would say the experiencing of this place grew to become a "silver lining." For me to live life from this modest place taught me that one needs not for the earthly possessions we all think we require every day. As it was, with nowhere to go but knowing that I had to take a step daily to make sure I was still alive, the silver lining philosophy was a healthy thought process by which to heal. I awoke daily in this place and felt, *I have to keep on going for my children.*

I give thanks to those who laughed with me, and at me, through these times. Caroyl, dear friend, who brought elegant sandwiches for us to nibble on as we sat on the floor of what I came to call my Italian oasis. I recall the day we sat watching the movie *Philadelphia* eating her sandwiches.

I give thanks to an Ethiopian mother whom I cared for one day as a nurse. She invited me to her family gatherings. She was from inner-city Oakland and she knew the answer. With large heart, she said, "Honey, fight for your children." To whom do you owe thanks?

From the knowledge of silver linings and from a position of self-love, we can work to re-establish what is important in life. Negative thoughts are turned into positive possibilities and laughter grows to become a healing source of light energy. Step by step, we begin to pave a path of recovery, celebrating each small success as it comes, embracing one positive word of encouragement and then another. We feed off of the positive and throw away negative things that bind us to the past.

We tunnel our energy and our vision in a way that rarely

makes sense to those around us. To others, we may appear to be acting as one without interaction, a reclusive hermit. There is a plan; stay the course always.

Continue in the tunnel and demand focus of yourself always. Others do not need to understand. In reality, their curiosity is nothing more than just that. Do not ever fuel the inquisitiveness of idle onlookers whose focus in life is to seek the negative. I do not imagine they have anything else to do.

There will always be a wide selection of more exciting things to do at the moment. It is the long-term vision and the devotion to the individual challenge which will get us to the top. These things take time, patience, and belief in oneself. And love of oneself. I thank my children for their unwavering presence. They possessed constant enthusiasm. They embraced each moment with honor and grace. When situations arose when my dreams for them were larger than the money we had in our pockets, they did not complain nor challenge the moment. They waited for me, knowing we were on track to create miracles. I owe these children, as my dreams for them often overtook the reality of our moments.

My upbringing provided me with the belief in myself to get through anything. I never shared with my proud family the course of events, losing my children. I knew they would not understand. Nor could I share with them the experience of nearly losing my freedom. I believe, in some regard, they were mentally there for me. Remembering their strength, and our past work ethic experiences growing up in Connecticut, I believed I could accomplish whatever I set my mind to.

My family began to pull away as the pain of the journey

intensified. When they saw me floundering, having lost it all, it was too much for them to understand. I believe now that I retreated into myself so as not to hurt them. I did not wish for them to experience the pain. I stopped calling and updating them of our news. The dedication I take to building my estate in the wilderness is nothing other than the devotion my parents took to their lives and businesses back east. We were meant to work hard and focus completely.

My memories of my childhood include my parents enjoying the day around the pool with a big family barbecue – only after the hard day's work was done. This was our tradition. We did not go far; we created our paradise at home.

My parents were positive life guides in their ability to tunnel their attention to building and accomplishing dreams for our family and for our future. They were immensely successful designers and florists. It was a hard act to follow. The challenge I was made to endure was just that, a temporary thing which I believe to have been a test of my character.

*We are never given more than we can handle. I suppose that for those of us given much to challenge us, the gods must believe we can handle all of it. I know without the challenge, I would not have had the full and eventful life I have been blessed to adventure. And so I am thankful.*

CHAPTER TEN

# Dedication to Heal and Empower Others

*Children do not ask to be maltreated; they grow to do as they "see." We live surrounded by societal stress which will unfortunately not change in the near term. We strive to find solutions as best we can; we care for and we heal others as best we can. "Tunnel Vision" is our solution to a horrible problem including abuse, neglect, hostile harassment, and long term individual suffering. "Tunnel Vision" works miracles. We know.*

**D**ifficult and overwhelming obstacles are inevitable. Sometimes they can be overpowering. First and foremost, allow yourself time and attention to grieve over the defeat. You are a gentle creature of the universe. You need to feel and experience the moment fully and completely and take in the process before moving on. Though it is never easy and never fair, it is your experience in life. Exercise your right to mourn and reflect. Allow yourself to find creative ways to nurture yourself and then give yourself permission to move on and create miracles.

One day you will arise whole. You may feel instinctively it is time to move on. You will have found a reason to move past the pain and sorrow. Whatever your reason, be committed to the creation of a state of mind and presence of spirit to proceed openly, ready to look at your present circumstances and take positive action. There are immense possibilities in finding and embracing success. There are huge opportunities to heal from violence and pain. Be of healthy body, mind, and spirit, to continually enrich yourself with strength and passion within your very being. Do not allow anyone else to think and act for you. Learn to speak, act, and be, with presence of spirit and lightness of action on your own. Your strength and commitment to life are not to be shaped by someone else's vision of how your life should be.

Empower yourself daily with words and actions affirming that you are a worthy being, justified to be successful and whole without abuse, trauma, and violence. Empower others by this process, most importantly, your children. Miracles are everywhere; dedicate yourself in tunnel vision focus to make all miracles happen. Awaken a spirit inside yourself with the energy and momentum that's yours for the asking. Become an example of peace and tranquility. This is all good for body, mind, and soul. Seek often to laugh and to smile.

Oberto took me to court, claiming that I was not paying child support. I believed Oberto should have been the one to have been punished and never imagined I would be challenged for not paying him more than what I had already given up. On a Friday morning, I was found to be guilty of eleven counts of contempt. Our judge announced I would be going to jail for six months. I had already had my life ripped from me. Jail was not an option. I worked all through the weekend, finding an attorney to represent me in court Monday morning where the charge was reduced to 700 hours of community service, my silver lining. Besides the avoidance of jail, the service is perhaps why I am, today, involved as docent, as volunteer, as nonprofit founder.

I expose my mistakes and weaknesses to share with you the humanity and humility of my life. I move on awkwardly, but with a bit of lighthearted humor. I tell stories which provide us with a wake-up call to keep us on track so that more extensive damage does not happen. Stories let us know we are not alone in our struggles. In stories, we share and collaborate. In storytelling we heal.

Tell your story. Awaken to enjoy life. Move from hatred and abuse to peaceful contentment. Choose to educate others to the horrible consequences caused by senseless trauma and violence. Choose to be dedicated to making peace. Choose not to see anger and pain. Choose only to see the dreams and miracles awaiting your experience of the moment. Magically, what you do not place energy on will go away.

I have come to an awakening, even with sanctions imposed on me and have learned that not everything in life is fair. I attempt to see only good and therefore yearn to experience my children every hour of every day in nurturing and loving ways. I have made the best of a situation that at best was limiting.

I take in life one moment at a time, for each and every moment is a gift. I do not crave for more, as life itself can be taken in an instant. I seek to embrace the big picture, to make dreams my reality. My desire – to see beyond and accomplish much in the future – will be played out tunnel-vision style. This is my own challenge. At some miraculous point of healing, a flame inside me reignited, setting fire to my soul long buried in sorrow. I learned, and now share with you the sorrow and the joy. No matter how complicated your story, stay steadfast, stand strong, continue to move forward. If you are challenged by loss and immobilized, know that there is a way out of the abyss, a way that can shape forward motion, a way that can ultimately be an inspiration for all.

I achieved for self and others (my lovely children) and continue to achieve in my focused, tunnel-vision way. And the ability to clearly and completely focus becomes easier every day. The task at hand is not about pain and suffering. It is not about what has come before. The path also has nothing to do with sympathy for there is no time. Once ignited, there is no emoting on this long and focused journey, only words about tomorrow. The time is now for clarity of purpose, for discipline, for focused tomorrows. Maintain a known and secure course, a determined picture in your mind.

Be selective in your goals as time is short and goals are many. Begin fresh and alive each day to see life with renewed excitement. Breathe deeply and stretch beyond the past. I begin each day in silent prayer, calling out to spirits to enlighten my path. Secure in actions and direction, I go forth, electrified with movement. I move through uncharted waters to victory. I climb, focusing my mind and my spirit. I march onward. You can, too. With necessary, purposeful steps you will succeed. Allow it to happen. Revel in the feelings of hope, solidly secured by actions, protected from the penetration of outsiders by the walls of the tunnel. Each action strengthens your resolve.

Look to those around you as guides to follow. Seek out the focused ones. Listen to the verse of others who live to inspire. Sarb created a blueprint, his version of the Taj Mahal. I watched him design and create his dream home. Sarb inspired me. Conversely, be wary of those who drain you of energy rather than inspire. I have spent time reflecting on moments wasted following people mindlessly and enabling them. Moments wasted on idle fancies, trivialities, champagne dreams. Time passes quickly, leading to emptiness on these paths.

Your tunnel will focus you, direct your moments in life, for yourself, for legacy, for children, for family. Your quest is enabled by life-defining vision. For my son Cedric, the clear focused voice of a child. Fight harder for me, Mom. Whom do you fight for? Healing means you're renewed, refreshed, revived. Healing means you are moving forward. Each of us has a sacred spirit filled with passion and able to challenge every obstacle, to withstand life's demons. Uncover your spirit. Go now, undaunted and unafraid. For given the chance, we can awaken the spirit within and become whole again.

Act and the road will open before you. Truth will appear faster than before. What you believe will become reality and progress will be made by sheer momentum. Move in thought and action and come to expect that which you seek. So it is that miracles happen. They are there right now if you can see and feel them. Move in harmony with the events around you. Move in harmony with the healing flow of the universe.

# CHAPTER ELEVEN

# Avoidance of Noise, Negativity, and Drama

*We must forever keep on, "Tunnel Vision"-style, dedicated to a more peaceful society for all. No abuse of any kind is right. Empowerment, nurturing, and love for all individuals will ensure a more productive and creative society. Think, act, and live, "Tunnel Vision."*

**B**e aware of your surroundings always. Know that what is done can never change. Events in the past affect the future course of everything that comes after. Move to take hold mentally and spiritually; the choice of how to wake in the morning, the choice of how to recover from daily drama and noise, is ultimately in your hands. Speak and act with control and dedication to think first and act after quiet reflection. Think, breathe, and then act.

Choose not to respond out of pity, self-doubt, or victimization. I remember the words of my youngest as I ventured out to secure our dreams. I was still fearful of the abuser who sought to have my freedom taken from me so as to further punish and immobilize me. My youngest son Zubin was calm and rational, not for one moment giving thought to paralyzing emotion. His words, my salvation: *Mom, get in, get out, and get on with it.*

Tragedy may cross your path, looking to take you from your course of action. Choose to make "tragedy" your friend – welcome it, nurture it, and then usher it aside. Laugh in the face of it. You are in a flow of movement that does not stop. Look always for the good in that moment, for if you do, you will find good. Nurture this movement; your timeline and commitment to success will overshadow the negativity of the pain. Do not nurture the drama that has befallen you.

Once you decide to move beyond tragedy and dedicate yourself to not giving it the energy others would wish for it to embrace, you will see how quickly the tragedy will pass and move on to find someone more willing to embrace it. Rejoice in your ability to rally in the heat of the moment and move onward. Throw away the violin; move on from the puddles of pity. Rise and announce to the world that an end to suffering will be assured. For each one of us to reach beyond the pain and immobility that has befallen us, we must choose to tunnel now and move on to heal. There is no other choice. Others will move as we move.

Move past drama. Yours is a glorious path and there will be no hardship or difficulty to endure if you believe this is so. Never look back in crafting your wonderful journey. With simple and perfect grace, move on towards the creation of the next step and then the next. Anything and everything is possible with clear and unobstructed vision and a totally committed focus void of the negative energy of pain, sorrow, and drama. This is your tunnel – a vividly imagined approach, no matter the charted course or obstacles that stand in your way.

In hindsight, I wonder what my youngest son would have said had he been present while his dad was throwing milk and clothes my way. I had come to pick up my babies; Oberto had screamed, attempting to scare me off. At the time, he was successful in his quest. Knowing my young son, he would have wanted me to welcome the experience. It is all in how we see the light. I breathe and embrace health and happiness now. I smile at the thought of my son's creativity.

My gift is for myself and my children. As I look up to the skies, I pray for my ex-husband, so that all of us may forever end the pain of persecution, arguing, and fighting, and move on. Doing so allows our children a view of life which they have not been fortunate enough to have growing up, a life filled with happiness and contentment. A life I desire is one where conflict does not rule, a life where family unity creates strength of character, a life of harmony with commitment to each other.

Many life lessons come to us along the way. Life is short, filled with unexpected tragedy. We know not what will happen each moment. Knowing this, I am moved to orient my actions to care for and support others rather than focus on acts of persecution and intolerance. I do not have the time nor the desire to anguish over things I cannot control nor wish to control. I have many more mountains to climb in the conquest of dreams. I have no need to give energy to those things behind me now. The universe did not intend for us to mold it and the beauty lies in differences among all of us. I pray for peace. I pray my children avoid all hostility and violence in their wonderful lives as best they can.

I acknowledge that my tunnel will allow no more time and attention to a past that seeks to hold me back in fear and sorrow. I have been blessed with the ability to move on from the pain that bound me tightly. Tunnel vision has become a metamorphosis of action from descriptive drama to healing affirmation. I remember the passion in my oldest son's voice when he told me to fight harder. This came to mean for me that I should also dream harder. My son was the first person ever to believe in me. What a wonderful thing love is. So much joy and success was brought to my son in his hour of pain that he turned the nurturing back upon his mother to aid in her healing. I am forever thankful for this gift.

In my darkest days, he announced his own quest for tunnel vision, achieving safety and success for himself. He was willing to testify on his own behalf in order to free himself and discover success. He then implored me to scale mountains I had never before climbed. I thrived in things that I never before felt I could accomplish. It was an awe-inspiring experience to have someone love and believe in me so much. I was applauded on to greatness by my son. I know that the ability to gain clarity of thought through the influence of tunnel vision has made the difference in my son's success and accomplishments. It has certainly made the difference in my life.

Experiencing my son's commitment did much to energize my visionary spirit and further assisted me in my continued personal focus to embrace the tunnel vision I needed to succeed for myself and for my other sons. Today, I continue to dream as each day before. When those around me thought I would fail, I stayed close to vision. Ending the drama means starting a sojourn of energy and soul power of the magnitude and strength that can move mountains. Jump higher, run faster, leap for joy!

End the drama and embrace and live tunnel vision. Recognize limitations, then call to action the movement of mountains. Find an experience, feel it, live through it day by day. Draw upon the experience and grow to accept what you have gone through. Reveal yourself to others. Laugh with others about your limitations. Communicate with your children the beauty of the simple things around you. Know and honor every moment of every day. Honor and care for others. What we say matters, how we think and what we do, even the small things. The effects of your words and your actions will follow you always. Know your boundaries. Watch patiently.

Assist others who have suffered loss and sorrow, help them form their tunnel, help them chart a course in the pursuit of accomplishing dreams, help them awaken to a new awareness of self. Allow others to experience their pain of loss. We should not be shielded from this reality. Love and comfort another in a time of need. Awaken to move forward clearly and with a commitment to pushing forward.

Self fulfillment is the reward for ending the drama and embracing the tunnel. The tunnel is both the means and ends for awakening each morning with certainty that you can accomplish all that you set to accomplish. Openly and enthusiastically acknowledge the power of self love and the ability to accomplish miracles. Once this is known, there is no turning back. Change will occur in the continued process and exploration of love for self, taking an account of this focus, one minute at a time and one day at a time. Change will unfold, as will clarity.

With clarity of thought comes clarity of action. Think of how this may work for you in your day to day life. Where might you need to go to accomplish this state of serenity to find yourself? Free yourself from the negative behavior patterns of thinking another will save you. Free yourself from negative self-thought, the poor-me thoughts, the no-way-out thoughts. Tunnel vision is not about these emotions. It's not about your baggage or itemizing your roadblocks. It's about forward action, forward motion, focused and centered attention. It's about the road to freedom.

CHAPTER TWELVE

# See the Big Picture

*Main points covered in this book include the importance of working to identify those children and families negatively affected by the trauma of violence as quickly as possible. The degree to which long-term violence and trauma have occurred directly affects the chance for a normal adult life without the critical intervention of "Tunnel Vision." The importance of educating professionals to acknowledge signs and symptoms of "silent pain" is addressed. This book speaks to the importance of being open and accepting of all forms of silver linings as they come one by one, of listening for hourly and daily cues. Daily hope for and achievement of progress from slow and consistent forward movement toward the eradication of personal destruction is the ultimate and impassioned goal.*

The coyote howls late into the night; we listen carefully to his call. An injured child cries out in pain from neglect, abuse; I am moved to act. Once trauma by violence is inflicted upon the soul of a child, deep scars are forever present. What is needed: We need to speak out, we need to acknowledge the damage caused to all the innocent among us. Each and every child must be held dear; silent victims with no ability to shield themselves from evil ways. We must pray that the protection of the injured will someday be assured. We must demand love, respect, compassion, and nurturing of all souls. The ability to live in peace, without abuse, is a universal right.

My Tunnel Vision story is one of pain and isolation. After fourteen years of silent reflection, my movement forward has brought me to a point of standing up and crying out, an awakening, a call to fight hard and not fail. This has become my mantra. No individual has a right to cage another individual spiritually or physically. We cannot allow ourselves to become silenced by the trauma of our tale, no matter how difficult our story may have been for us as we have lived it. I share my ordeal as a possible guide to follow, yes. But also to raise awareness, so others may realize the damage caused to human life in the hands of a system unaware and unprepared. The goal is to protect the innocent. Courts continue to make callous and biased decisions. Abusers are allowed to manipulate the system, with custody of small children awarded to calm and calculating manipulators.

Defense attorneys close their eyes to violence. Exceedingly smart individuals become willing to do injustice to "win" for their clients. They turn off their emotions to achieve a victory, not stopping to see the effect on an innocent child or children. The end societal goal must be to achieve a state of affairs where no child and no parent will have to experience the suffering children and parents currently must often endure.

A known fact: three infants were taken from a mother, placed into the arms of a documented "culturally high-strung," "violent individual" with a propensity for "rage reactions." It was noted, physicians would not allow the abuser into their offices. It was well-documented; counselors noted dangerous behavior and threats to persons when the individual in question believed someone was interfering with his ability to control the situation. Judgment cast, my life changed forever. I was never allowed again to legally sleep with my infant children.

Like the many cases that came before mine, I was pigeonholed as "emotional," to fit a mold meant to ease the burdens of backlog and turmoil within the family court domestic dispute system. It's difficult for family court to deal with emotional accusations. And so it's exceedingly common for infants and small children to be placed with known violent, *non*-emotional, seemingly calm, seemingly rational individuals – those individuals whose sole focus is to manipulate and control the outcome, versus someone devoted to caring and nurturing victim children. The manipulator and the courts essentially punish the emotional parent. It's the failure of the system and an injustice for all.

Overly emotional mothers do not win custody of children. Calm, educated fathers with calculating power gain control, get even, win. I would come to see the children unscheduled; my sons called and asked for me, crying, demanding my presence. It never occurred to me that the police would be summoned. That I would be scorned, Oberto utilized each vulnerable episode against me. I did not come from a position of control. I was otherwise an emotional mess with no focus or direction. Constant struggle can cause permanent damage to children needing collaborative parenting. I know full well the damage that can be done.

We need only to look to society to see the effects of this abuse on the injured. Insecure young adults seeking love and respect, yet unsuccessful in achieving it, add to the grave statistics we see in the juvenile system and add to the growth in gang violence. I am moved to cry out for future generations of children affected by callous decisions of a court system eager to move on and settle cases in haste, without due consideration for circumstances. Facts matter and must be considered in each and every circumstance. Individuals matter and precedent cannot always lead the way to justice. Never before has there been an outcry of this magnitude to stop abuse against innocent children. Since the early 1990s, courts have utilized a methodology of choosing the non-emotional party to become the custodian. This tactic was deemed more time-efficient as opposed to dealing with more emotional scenarios. Courts, not remaining engaged after a judgment is rendered, are often unaware of the long-term damage.

I share a story of one family's struggle – a family torn apart by an uninformed and uncaring judicial system. Stories such as this one affect our hearts and souls. They are not, sadly, uncommon. Collectively, they reveal an injustice that must be heard. No more can lives be affected by abuse, neglect, or violence. Change must happen – one story at a time, one family at a time, one person at a time, one infant at a time. Hostility and control by the abuser is embraced and used by the court, played out against the non-violent party in a way that drives the innocent to a place of isolation and immobility. Punishment rendered by the court against the accuser, and by the abuser against the accuser, leads to emptiness and despair, infant children taken and "owned" by another.

Banished from infant children, delegated a new responsibility – to pay for the injustice, wages garnished – I turned the house deed over to my ex-husband, in despair, fearful of his threats to take my four infant children back to his country. Most who knew us would disbelieve our tale, choosing not to listen to our cries for assistance, hoping, perhaps, that the cries would go away. They must have thought there had to be something terribly wrong with me psychologically. People wished to disbelieve the court had granted custody to the abusive party. The common thread: What is wrong with her that she did not get her children?

Others sat motionless, in shock, and telling me not to worry, I would get my children and my justice, as though my loss and pain was transitory, even illusionary. Many encouraged me to wait for a miracle, hoping that the problem would disappear. Others terrified and numb to the assistance that was necessary were shocked at the damaging physical and psychological outcome.

I cried myself to sleep, imagining little children clinging to the corners of their beds for safety. My second son Alessio, a gentle artistic soul, experienced a period of shock, unable to learn the alphabet due to "auditory deficit discrimination." His mind shut out all episodes of yelling and violent rage to shield him from pain. Years later, he shared some of his journal entries with me. He had grown to believe the only one to care for him was himself.

Some effects of long-term abuse may be clear immediately. It is, however, much more common for the worst effects to emerge much later. Cries for help, emotionalism, acting out in maladaptive patterns of behavior may be seen by an untrained professional as truant activities. We may punish a child inadvertently, when in fact the cause and effect of damage was initiated by a violent and abusive parent or other party. What's needed now is a system of justice in which facts, however emotional, are embraced, where violence is minimized and ownership of children and adults as a form of abuse and manipulation is eliminated.

No child deserves to live a life of isolation from the love of an adoring parent. No child should live in an abusive situation by the hands of the court. It becomes crucial for a child in a troubled family unit affected by trauma and harassment, to maintain a sense of self and stability while going through traumatic scenarios. The technique of tunnel vision can assist in establishing mentally and "for real" a forward flow from victimization effects of violence to self-motivated sufficiency to move on and thrive.

Without forward flow and careful and consistent intervention, children and adults are injured psychologically and immobilized physically for the long term, causing irreversible pain and destruction to the individual and the family unit. To create movement in the system, change must be demanded. We must insist on zero-tolerance for any and all violence. The damage is too great and affects a nation in emergent need of change.

The injury to human lives will ripple on if we do not work now to halt all abuse against the innocent. Statistics reveal the horrific findings about prisons filled with individuals injured in large part from some physical or psychological event during childhood. On one occasion, a prisoner stated to me, "I had a hard life." How many of the "life" inmates could have been nurtured one more day by someone devoted to their welfare?

How better would this world be with a bit more love and guidance prior to destructive events occurring to cause a human to be locked up forever?

Our fast-paced culture lacks love for the family unit and the individual in the materialism that surrounds us. Hurting children and love-starved infants soon become adults with dormant feelings of pain and loss. They haven't received the attention and consistent mentoring required to learn the importance of care and nurturing of a trusting soul. The family system in our country shows signs that something is gravely wrong. The courts are to blame for handing over children to those we *know* have abusive tendencies. We must work to systematically heal those affected by violent behavior. We must heal souls damaged by lack of values and support before it is too late and more innocent souls are meant to suffer.

On my son's urgent request, I challenged a court who had denied my fight for justice on so many occasions. With my son behind me this time, I felt more clear, determined, and focused. I recall the feeling we would not accept "no." We lost the first time, having been denied the ability to make use of my son's simple eloquent truth to testify in court. But in our mentality of tunnel vision, we pressed onward, speaking to the best interests of children.

We filed again, this time being granted an *ex parte* exception to allow the testimony of my son to be heard. He testified on his own behalf in front of his father. My son deserved all that was awarded to him, the right to live in peace and harmony without abuse and trauma. He is a stronger person for his honesty and his conviction to justice.

When I teach neonatal resuscitation, one message is clear. There is only one golden moment to act. It is all we have. To save a baby's life, to stop the potential of brain damage, one must act deliberately and swiftly and with total focus. There is a procedure that is necessary for the best outcome. So it is with tunnel vision – focus and concentration, deliberate and certain. This is not a dress rehearsal. This is life. Begin the challenge of tunnel vision with total commitment to moving forward. Be clear and deliberate in accomplishing your goals. You can reach your dreams. Collectively, as a society, we can accomplish much more when we choose to care.

# CHAPTER THIRTEEN

# Techniques for Survival Day by Day

*We have formulated a master plan of "Tunnel Vision" to shield the individual affected by trauma by stepping in and providing "Tunnel Vision"-style focus, imagination, and coping mechanisms as well as personal nurturing skills to make a difference on a daily basis. This mechanism of focus, nurturing, and dedication to the self, will aid immensely in the coping mechanism and the ability to move toward post-trauma and post-abuse. The past experience of daily violence and harassment witnessed and experienced does not simply disappear; it is part of the individual's life tape, long-term. Utilizing "Tunnel Vision," individuals will embrace this disciplined and focused methodology; they will think, breathe, and speak a fresh and life-invigorating pattern of behavior, to survive and thrive.*

When you are isolated in a downward spiral it becomes overwhelming. Today I ache over the things done and decisions made. Time does not repeat itself; I cannot get back the precious moments where others made decisions for my children. Harsh and tragic decisions of the court – removing a mother from the life of an infant – result in fearful children left to fend for themselves in corners of bedrooms. The damage is not always immediately apparent, but we can imagine the shock and devastation emerging somehow, someday. For my part, my children and I grew to embrace the silver linings of our isolation. No one completely understood the unusual events or behavior patterns except us, living close to the tragedy day to day. We were open and accepting as we dealt with our fate.

But it was calming to have friends at least look beyond the insanity of the moment to sometimes say in all sincerity, "I understand what you must be going through." These were unique visions of our difficult times during which many chose instead to think unusual and crazy and disturbed thoughts about who we *really* were and how we had gotten ourselves into the mess we were in. For those who supported me, I remain grateful for the genuine, thoughtful, nurturing comments. I am not at all sure I would have been as clear in my thinking had not the occasional angel, clothed as a friend, not paved our way with moments of hopeful thoughts and rescue remedies.

As a result of my actions or inaction, I was forced to live with the consequences of my not-very-well-thought out plans. My ignorance of the legal system, subordination, lack of self-conviction, and over-emotional state cost me dearly. But having my children taken was far beyond the price to pay for the crime of ignorance. I was told I had no ownership interest of these children. I was told to go away. My ex-husband informed the schools and neighbors I was no longer involved, that he "owned" the children. I stopped receiving mail regarding my children and the preschool assigned to take my children was told I was not allowed to get my babies. So began the years and years of battles that divorce attorneys live to unjustly advocate for, and families get financially and emotionally destroyed over. Witness the traumatic destruction of small victims during this emotionally charged charade.

It was impossible for me to have focused forward movement in my life. I found I had no energy to maintain the legal continuance of the fight from either an emotional or financial standpoint. I made a decision counter to my attorney's advice. I signed over all rights to our house believing this "gifting" to my ex-husband of our home would not only provide stability for my children, it would also prevent my ex-husband from returning to his home country. I had no more cash to fight with. I had no more energy to continue the war. I was physically, psychologically, and financially broken. I needed to start somewhere and I saw this as a first step, handing over the house.

The decision at least allowed my young gentle children the ability to stay in the same house they'd lived in since birth, in a safe and secure neighborhood. Had I demanded to keep half the house, I knew I would have to sell it. Knowing the determination and control of my ex-husband, I could not fathom this. With the acquisition of the house and the assets, my ex-husband gained enormous personal power and domination over me. This had nothing to do with the health and safety of my children. I now believe I wasted valuable emotional time in my attempts to win the case. I didn't possess the legal finesse required, nor did it seem anyone cared to examine the facts of the case. The die had been cast. I know my ex-husband was fearful to the point of desperation of losing his children.

He wanted to get even with me. The courts should have been thoughtful enough to have worked things out in order to benefit the children, rather than one angry parent. In the end, my children suffered. Perhaps the courts were afraid of my ex-husband as well, thinking it best to give him his way.

From scars, we are held back from experiencing life in a way that can be full and enriching. But from mistakes, through our pain and trauma, we must find a way to heal and move on with grace. If we hear ourselves continually playing a violin, crying in pain, we learn this action accomplishes nothing. We attempt to stop how we react to our pain and re-program ourselves to move beyond this hurt one day at a time if not for self, then for our children. We must love our children totally and completely.

If we hear others anguishing over loss and sorrows of the past, not moving anywhere, we understand the importance of pushing on to write a different story and incorporate some kind of miracle into the narrative for ourselves and for our children. Life is too short to stay behind, only feeling pain, isolation, and pity for self. Having seen the glory in the creation of miracles, I am motivated to act with enthusiasm to nurture others. A caution from my own experience.

If we seek to have another heal us by grabbing onto his coattails, we become absorbed into that person's life and lose perspective on our own. Eventually, we will see that their passion and destination is not what fulfills us. It's okay to befriend and love another dearly and completely; however we must allow our inner voice to emerge with gentle grace and without restrictions. We must always seek to find that, in relationships, the best strength is to be ourselves.

Even in the midst of the fear that binds us, we must act on our own for recovery to be real. In healing, we push ourselves to love ourselves and thus learn about our needs, perhaps for the first time. While I enjoyed hanging on to coattails and found it stimulating, I found I enabled others to better the successes of their own endeavors. In the end, their concerns were taken care of but I was in exactly the same place I had been before. After living to suit schedules and designs of others, the routine without commitment did not form the basis for a relationship. I was left feeling I had lost myself and had neglected attending to my growth, unique design, and individual passions.

I ultimately decided I would never again allow another to rule my destiny. I would instead challenge myself to reach beyond the torture that had come my way and to never let another squash the spirit within me. I would dare to dream big and accomplish much. I would aspire to tunnel vision.

Among other things, this meant I would allow the truth to prevail, and fight to maintain my individuality. I would battle against any and all allegations against me and win. All of my hours and attention would go into building my dreams for the future. I acted with tunnel vision – a sincere dedication to empower myself to move past anything which would have before stood in the way. I am moved to continue to shelter and mentor my children. I embrace them like sheep. Like cherubs, I call out for the angels to guide their gentle souls from the evils of the past.

A temper out of control and without defined boundaries is an extremely dangerous weapon. A hot temper wields incredible power, manipulating all in its path. I allowed this type of anger a potent strength beyond which it deserved. And I, in turn, became emotionally out of control. The best remedy for this situation would have been silence. I was not properly in tune with how to handle abusive and verbally hostile individuals. I did not have insight necessary to stay calm, to cope more effectively with patterns of hostile behavior. I needed to have thought more in terms of the cultural background of the individual or the patterns of behavior of the culture from where the abusive person had come.

I wish I had been coached, mentored, to say the right things at the right moment for my survival, to process the situation more objectively. Ultimately, I was not able to withstand the ongoing threats and hostility. My psyche, absent emotional support, failed and I lost my personal ground. My body reacted as well. I developed respiratory and skin sensitivities to stress. Because I was not able to deal successfully with the abusive behavior, it spilled out into how my children reacted within the environment. I saw painful reactions to perceived violent behavior patterns in the eyes of my small children. The fear I saw in their response to the scenarios of ongoing trauma hurt me more. I was quick and impulsive in my actions, as I felt more and more out of control.

During my lengthy legal proceedings I learned much too

late the importance of playing by the rules, of what it meant to be obedient to the system. The way I managed my affairs was not looked upon kindly by the court. The court is in control. I learned something that will last me lifetimes: humility. The court system, it must be noted, is in many ways incapable of change. Finding ways to avoid the system and, more importantly, uncovering methods to creatively deal with those in your life without legal intervention is advisable. For my part, I remain non-litigious.

I will not seek to offend anyone. My goal is in healing my family and those interested in finding the miracles in life that are graciously awaiting them. Think in this restorative fashion and the energy and grace surrounding this way of life will certainly come to meet you. Entertain good thoughts – like attracts like. I will forever seek to find the peace for others in pain as I sought our own salvation from pain and suffering. Trauma happens, sometimes without warning. Our hair is pulled, our clothing ripped, we suffer terrible bruises. For a while, we go numb and choose to ignore the violent scenario. Out of fear, we become afraid, emotional, and subservient to the one inflicting trauma upon us. We apologize to the abuser. I cannot now imagine why. But here starts the circle. The question arises: If you are being abused, and if you cannot deal with the situation, then why do you stay? Because what we are used to on a daily basis comforts us.

Our children see violence. It is impossible to escape the pain they experience, written in their beautiful eyes. Their injured souls, stunned by the acts of violence, struggle to survive. We see this in actions, we feel it. Others, peripheral to our situations, have no idea of the history which caused our ongoing weakness and immobility and the emotions and actions of our children. Outsiders may characterize our immobility as a clinical condition or say we are lazy or careless. It is impossible for outsiders to fully understand violence and the life events surrounding life-altering trauma. If we stay in an abusive situation, we are misunderstood and our motives are questioned. If we leave, we are probed after our loss.

Due to the subtle complexities of our situation, we see no way out, defenseless, subordinating to the abuser. We pray for some miracle to save us. We reach a point in either sickness or mental anguish where the need to save ourselves and our children is of paramount importance and so we run. Immense pain and long-term damage are caused by repeated acts of violence toward a child or anyone in harm's way. A strange attraction takes hold of a previously strong person to the violent person, as the closeness shared in one moment can blind us from repetitive verbal assaults.

Our children suffer as the focus within the relationship is on the pain and the possible return **of** another trauma. Gone are normal boundaries. In its place – one cycle of cruelty after another. We plead with the abuser to stop the constant acts of aggressiveness and control. Unfortunately, cycles of traumatic abuse continue unabated, breaking us down. The intent of the aggressor is to scare, then to harm us, further breaking down our confidence and ability to think we can move on. If this all sounds familiar in your life, then you know that cycles of abuse, violence, and trauma work a destructive magic on the mental and physical being. Illness sets in as the system is shocked again and again. From a societal standpoint, these signs of physical and mental distress must be recognized by trained professionals and immediate referrals must be made.

In my experience, long after an episode, there was always an apology and a promise for new beginnings and "this will never happen again." I cannot recall how many times episodic outbursts occurred followed hours later with "I will never do this again." Most troubling is that the events became more and more commonplace, with the abusive individual continuing to seek control and domination. I recall my heart racing out of control after one brutal encounter. I recall my baby at my breast, hoping and praying the abuser, who had been raging out of control, would not return. I hoped I would not have to deal with the sensation of terror ever again.

Those of us affected by violence desire to hide away from the possibility of injury. This is not a temporary condition, but a lifestyle, as the act of getting close to someone reminds us of situations when we have been taken advantage of in a violent fashion. We lose the ability to trust others in an intimate and long-term relationship. We bury ourselves in projects, so as not to be hurt again. To emerge from this life condition of subordination and pain systematically weakening our ability to care for self and others, we must learn to care for ourselves. We must move positively to trust again and, as individuals, become healthy and social to survive.

In our search for self-fulfillment and during our mission for self-exploration apart from violence, we separate from the abusive past. This allows us to lighten our load, to step away from haunting conditions and to learn one baby step at a time to participate in the joys of life, without persecution or verbal torment. No one should go through life expecting bruises and scratches nor should one anticipate verbal abuse. A choice to move forward, once executed, may be filled with unusual consequences. We must deal with these costs and know this is all part of the master plan. Lessons are to be learned from each step along the way. All experiences are valuable and teach us important life lessons about ourselves and others.

How I healed took a steadfast daily focus on the simple things. I had to stop listening to the noise; I had to stop caring about judgment. I taught Cedric about silver linings. I enrolled him in a new school in all advanced placement classes where none of the past was known. He immediately took on a new identity minus the scorn that had befallen him. I drove him to L.A. for a two-week road trip, staying at nice places, looking at colleges. I believe part of why I sold my condo was to have the funds to give more, be more with him in the moment. We together did many things so that I gave him little time to be alone. Yet I did not cage his thoughts or actions.

When he experienced panic attacks I believed him and took him immediately to the E.R. Funny, one time there was another young boy in the E.R. for the same reason. Seeing the other boy going through the same symptoms was helpful. Together we look ahead calmly and diligently one baby step after another. Going through this with my son made it easier for me to accomplish my own miracles. My job at the time was amazing. Mary my boss said, "Take care of your son."

Days with my son driving nowhere in particular, past the discomfort of not knowing what to say, until words came naturally. Then there was pizza, counseling, whether he benefitted from this time or not, we went. Every day I made special. The acts were simple, not life-changing, but I shared time and more time and then some more. I acted straight from the heart, not from blame. That is what tunnel vision is all about; time, more time, and more time and so much listening and attention. When Cedric said, "Fight for me mom," what he meant was that I could not allow myself to lose. There was no choice but to win for both of us. What he gave us was the Tunnel Vision Approach. Thank you, Cedric.

CHAPTER FOURTEEN

# Healing our World

*For the individual looking to clarify, find focus and meaning, and simplify the complexity of a life post-stress and post-violence, for the professional counselor seeking to assist a child and family who seem lost and perhaps caught within a violent abusive atmosphere or in the memories of this experience, and for the attorney and court system who seek to more fully understand the plight of the individual and explore further the psychology behind domination and violence cycles, a "Tunnel Vision" approach takes you to a place beyond the study of the illness of manipulation and violence to a place encouraging strength of character and commitment to personal growth and miracle fulfillment. The ultimate goal for each individual is a full recovery of body, mind, and spirit, which includes healthy living and healing both physically and mentally. Life is a gift not to be destroyed and not to lack meaning and self-fulfillment.*

I listen to other parents who are now going through the pain I suffered years ago. I am saddened to see there has been no improvement in the process. An unreasonable amount of money is spent on attorney fees and court appearances. It's a waste of the court's time to deal with divorce cases where cycles of abuse are perpetuated with custody being granted to the aggressor.

Change is not forthcoming and injured children are growing up bearing the scars of the legal system's failures. The presiding justice may lack compassion and strength to seek fairness for injured parties as there are time constraints. On one occasion, our judge decided not to even hear our emotional story, though it had a direct bearing on an issue at hand. Once this judge granted me full legal and physical custody of my eldest son, years later, I thought better of him. It showed, at least on this one occasion, that he had listened to what my son had to say about abuse. He heard my son and acted accordingly.

Judge Porsche granted his decision based on evidence detailing, in part, "the best interest for the child" here, the father disowned his own son. After years of tragic injury, years sanctioned by the court without a mother's care and gentle nurturing, my son was granted a win. One would have thought, at that point, that a reasonable judge would be moved by my son's testimony to consider a judgment to protect my other children. The case closed; the custody rights for the other children were not deemed factors here. The law allows for no thought process of rational transference beyond what is written on the paper in front of the judge. We speak of the law not of righteousness of spirit. Be clear of the action you bring, act accordingly, and know the law.

My children suffered pain and psychological damage. I married a person with tendencies of outbursts. Unfortunately, his controlling behavior continued after the children were born. I only wish I could have been able to find a way to have dealt with the situation and to not have allowed a court system to rule the state of our affairs. No one is capable of making decisions that benefit children like the family.

To create a movement forward of such magnitude to move mountains, the problem of trauma against children and families as a result of decisions of the courts has to be openly exposed for all to see. Injured children must be identified and provided the chance to be nurtured freely and openly.

Laws need to be changed. Grants must be awarded to move us forward to ensure a non-violent society. Violence of any kind against children and victims must not be tolerated. This compassion must be extended societally. It is crucial to identify children and families negatively affected by the trauma of violence.

The importance of educating professionals to acknowledge signs and symptoms of silent forms of pain and trauma cannot be overemphasized. A place to start is with each child teaching and mentoring self-love. Allowing all children to write, to have a voice and to feel they are being listened to is key.

We may start compassionately with the "Tunnel Vision Approach", shielding out the noise, selecting those individuals affected by trauma and rage by stepping in and providing a focus, with imagination and coping mechanisms. The idea is to mentor individuals to move on and effectively make a difference in their lives. This mechanism of focus, clarity, and dedication to self, aids immensely in increasing coping skills for successful living.

What's important for us to realize, though they may not be there at all times, past experiences of violence and harassment do not disappear; the memories of traumatic episodes become a part of one's life tape. By implementing a Tunnel Vision methodology, an individual can embrace a disciplined and focused way of thinking, breathing, acting, and speaking in a renewed and invigorating pattern.

From within the tunnel, one can be taught to love self, one can learn to shield one's self from pain, numb away the past, embrace a more positive energy pattern to move forward successfully. With strength and determination, individuals are no longer tied to the power and manipulation of abuse that once bound them to fear.

Uncertain parenting scenarios are created by domestic battles. Young children question what will happen to them. They may feel guilt regarding the actions around them. It is imperative to have counseling and support systems available immediately. It is crucial to have the mother and father involved with the children in a non-hostile, non-violent way. It is vital for individuals affected by abuse to maintain a sense of self and stability. It is critical for a child to experience unconditional love. Should the nurturing of children and infants not be possible in a civilized manner due to the selfish interests of the feuding parents, then punishments should be levied. At stake: the heart, mind, and soul of a child.

One must have clarity and dedication to stop the long-term effects of hurt to children. Children were born of a united bond; so, too, should be the plan for their continued nurturing.

Unchecked, trauma and abuse cause devastating, dangerous, and debilitating consequences. The child must continue to establish bonds of trust and open communication. The child must be continuously loved and supported by both parents, and not isolated by the selfish needs of the parent seeking to dominate and punish the other parent.

Children are not pawns. The future of the child and no less than society are at stake. There are serious global consequences to violence that remains unchecked. How have we as a society allowed this situation involving the abuse and isolation of young children to remain unimpeded for as long as we have? Though there are recent efforts to review what is going on within the family court system, results are not happening fast enough.

Zero tolerance of any and all trauma to children by way of manipulation and active abuse and destruction must become the norm. Violence is a life condition. Society is attracted to violence. We hear about it in the news. We see it on television. It is nurtured in gangs as a way of life. Once inside the gang, violence binds individuals together. Should one try to leave a gang, death is the outcome.

We mentor our children to live a life of nonviolence. Our country stands firm that we adhere to a policy in schools of zero-tolerance to any type of violence. But recent legislation gives mixed messages as we legalize ownership of guns while dealing daily with gun killings. Every day we are subjected to traumatic violence of nation against nation. Young cadets are sent off to war in foreign lands. Young men return home haunted by the bodies of young men left behind. Violence changes people. When a troubled teenager walks into a high school and shoots young, innocent classmates, many suffer. Lives taken in senseless and traumatic killings have a deeper meaning than the momentary thrill of murder.

In a recent episode of road rage, a young father driving his sons on the highway was shot in the head and died with his sons by his side. There was no cause to define the incident. The children are left forever bruised by what they saw. Babies born to mothers on drugs with no way to provide for them perpetuate another growing epidemic. At birth there is always the fear of danger and abandonment should these babies be sent home with these moms. Child protective services with a job to monitor all situations harmful to a child all of the time, may overlook the one person who bears watching. These innocent children grow up without a mechanism by which to deal with life in a nonviolent way.

Senseless violence and brutality are the roots of further undoing of our basic family values. We recognize this by the number of cases filed within the family court system for domestic violence each and every day. The implementation of tunnel vision will re-establish a nurturing bond and worthiness of spirit to a scared, hurting, and lost soul unsure of what will happen next, especially one who has suffered repeated episodes of trauma.

Others must at once become empowered to understand the imminent harm violence and trauma have over time on an individual and a family unit. It is crucial there be an immediate intervention, and consistent follow-up sessions of healing involvement. We hope violent individuals open their eyes to see the damage they have caused before it is too late. Perhaps these individuals were never loved as children. The presence of violence perpetuates the same behavior in children who soon grow to repeat the same activity. Therefore, great sanctions must be imposed against those found to be abusive towards children. Terror and cruelty cannot rule. Children must not be managed by fear, verbal belittling, and ridicule.

Repeated violent destructive behavior causes horror and negative energy, stopping the creativity of the mind. Sickness and mental injury follow unchecked violent patterns. If the child is fortunate to get out of abusive surroundings, steps must be taken immediately to assess the potential damage.

All children must be enabled to get out or at least find ways to cope effectively with their ongoing caged conditions. If injured souls are challenged to move away from violence, at first they may appear as caged animals, afraid to move out of the cage. If they see clearly to their escape, thus allowing themselves to feel the nurturing graces surrounding their beings, they may be able to put an end to the flow of destructive patterns previously affecting them.

A renewed love for self will in turn allow silver linings to lead those affected in unique and inspiring ways. They will move with discipline and dedication to heal. From damage can arise miracles.

The fact is that violence in our society occurs most often behind closed doors. Ongoing abuse and the use of another for one's personal design occur to the point that normal functioning and social interaction with others becomes impossible. Trust in normal human contact is lost and the innocence of life itself is broken down. The individual can feel caged and defenseless, feeling it is best to do as he or she is told, or else.

Strive always to teach your children harmony and peace for each other. Support and mentor your children through whatever life challenges come their way. Seek to understand your child's uniqueness and work to bring it out. Be there and nurture them to greatness whoever they are.

Our world will be a better place for this. To decide against violence means to be committed to healing self and all other individuals affected. Once trauma and violence take hold, a sense of focus on child nurturing may be lost due to the all-encompassing nature of the vicious interludes. Ironically, this is the time children most need love, kindness, security, and nurturing.

The world as they know it is falling apart around them.

# CHAPTER FIFTEEN

# To Mothers and Fathers

*The experience of "Tunnel Vision" is unique and honestly personal. The story of "Tunnel Vision" reveals an emotional and moving real-life story of pain and vulnerability. We are moved to question how manipulation, violence, and abuse were "allowed" to overcome our ability to control a peaceful outcome. We must look deeply within our own psyche and background to see why or on what basis we adults "allowed" violence to happen. Children are innocent victims. The cycle of violence, if allowed to continue, will seek to perpetuate itself again and again and again. My youngest son taught me best, "Mom, simply stop talking." Is that all it would have taken to have lived without the violence? Children need to be nurtured. Be forever mindful of your precious children, your garden of children who are encouraged with guidance and love every day of their lives. Handle your cherished children with tender love, dignity, and respect. Acknowledge the differences in each of your children and teach them they are all miracles to be adored.*

Show your children the power of discipline, focus, and clarity of thought. This is found to cultivate simple self-awareness and a spirit of creativity. Instruct them to not feel hatred for others nor speak in a fashion of disrespect. Patterns of unkindness come back to haunt. My children never asked to be abused or isolated from an adoring mother. The actions of the court made one parent the custodian owner with the other parent made to bear the injustice. Unfortunately, abused and violated children often seek out behaviors they were raised to emulate, behaviors of violence and trauma.

Society looks at children who act out in pain not knowing what has happened to them over the years. People seek to quickly define the child for the sake of time, before moving on, however awkwardly. The child is defined essentially by precedent, and we go on to the next trauma case. The sad reality must be discovered and revealed. Most often, however, time constraints do not allow for this observation to occur. Most court decision-makers lack necessary psychological experience regarding long-term psychological effects, either on a child deprived of a parent, or a parent denied the child.

Children taken from one parent early in life and denied critical years of encouragement and support from that parent can show signs of shallowness, hidden so as not to display their emotions at all. They hide, appearing to be strong and unaffected, often times building up walls and not allowing others in.

Children who are not provided daily emotional sustenance and support with a parent dedicated to their needs become starved for guidance and affection. And it comes back to haunt years later in the form of baggage carried throughout life. Other children, who possess keen survival skills, learn early on not to rock the boat. These children disconnect from the non-custodial parent so as not to be seen as siding with anyone but the abuser. They appear happy, but are guarded and wary.

Countless mothers experience the loss of their children. Society is not kind in its judgment of our loss, often assuming the worst. What kind of mother must I have been to have lost my children? Self-worth, without the role of motherhood, crumbles. It's really a fight for all women who have gone through the loss of being allowed to be a mother. There is no cure for this loss. Time lost can never be replaced. I pray for and reach out to all mothers at this moment who have found themselves in a same or similar situation as I found myself. But peace will follow if you hold true to your ideals. I implore all mothers to look kindly upon the individual silver linings that surround you. In pain, we may find things that add strength and character to our lives. Emerge courageous, steadfast, and stronger, ready to assist another in pain.

We are challenged to move forward following traumatic life experiences. Through thick and thin, never give up. Always allow the sparkle, shine, and mystery of life to come through. This results in an energy outweighing all others. Children, aware of the fullness and peace that nurturing brings to their life, crave it. This is a healthy response. My eldest son, given an opportunity to recognize this need, screamed out to be given the right to consistently stay close to healing energy. To have achieved this for my eldest son was a miracle.

Children as caged animals are often not aware of the feeling of being loved. They become used to receiving little or no response to a tearful episode late in the night, void of a mother's kiss. Children need to believe in rainbows and moon-beams, not angry tirades. They need to believe there is always someone supportive and loving there for them. To have a full and complete impact on a life with the methodology we call tunnel vision requires getting inside the tunnel literally and staying there until you achieve your dream. There is no wiggle room and no way out once a goal has been voiced. Life choices are clearly in front of you.

Passionate goals for miracles and a loving commitment to self, with a burning desire of clarity and focus are the guiding principles of the journey. Possess a clear and total methodology of focus in the way you act and speak. The tunnel has been en-tered, there is no turning back. What is it that you are ready to commit to at this moment of your life?

If you are aiding another, you must consistently assist in the healing process. The injured person must want to be healed. It is through a showering of love and care to those af-fected that we show them a way other than trauma and pain. The process, a two-way flow, is never forced, but is dynamic. This is how my son responded to the process. He was ready to move on.

An intensity of connectedness between the affected per-son and the helper is greatly needed. The process involves total commitment and discipline. It entails communication and writing. It requires trust and caring. There is nothing forced. One cannot pull away once the process has begun. It is both enlightening and scary to be faced with such responsibility of commitment. There is no other choice; this must be recognized and the process continued for as long as it takes. A troubled person used to neglect and abuse long-term may not open up to nurturing right away. They may, in fact, deny their need for assistance, even in cases where it was initially requested.

The problem is that the atmosphere of respect and love the helper is offering is not the environment the victim has grown to experience as their natural habitat. But one must nevertheless go in the light of love and encouragement to somehow, and some way, hit a chord of acceptance and respect for the individual that the individual may never have experienced. This is when the true discovery process begins. One must be one-hundred percent committed to the process. One must consistently show and share love and support.

A reception to the guidance provided will occur once the former victim feels safe and respected as a person. They'll eventually develop some limited eye contact with you and the ability to talk about themselves. One day, you'll hear something that sounds like they are opening up to their feelings. For this, some boundaries will have been let down.

This is the *aha!* moment you've been looking for. I saw in my son, who screamed out a willingness to go through the process, a transformation in magnitudes no one would have ever expected or believed. It was a miracle unfolding in front of my eyes. I recall the movement away from pain to the introduction of simple actions which allowed my son to build confidence each day. I was questioned by others why I tried so hard to stand up for someone who had gone so low and, as they had put it (not understanding my son's way of crying for help), had "gotten into trouble." The answer was clear and easy: a belief in, a commitment to, an intense love for, and an opportunity to assist in healing someone at risk.

The sequence of events was something not completely within my son's control. I believe something greater than all of us was at work to find a way for my son to be back with me. Tunnel vision, a learned behavior of focus and skill, reduces the perpetuation of trauma and self-victimization. The approach and straightforward methodology encourages the spirit and provides the quiet space to cherish love for the soul, gently directing the individual to aid in nurturing self-respect and compassion for others.

Guided interaction leads to a more stable and violence-free life for the affected child and family members. Genuine acceptance of and love for self on a regular basis is a condition we need to be whole individuals. With the implementation of tunnel vision, we can achieve self-acceptance and grow to become more stable and passionate people with a core belief in the importance of nurturing spirits. Looking forward, what will the repercussions of the past do to mold the future of my children?

Tragedy has shown me to teach my children that from every challenge can bloom dreams and new creation. I started with a tunnel in mind. I wanted so much beyond the tunnel, but I continued onward slowly, monitoring and guiding my progress. Baby steps have guided and directed my actions. I face any and all challenges with care, so as to see possibilities and learning experiences. I am focused on the creative pursuit of silver linings in all I see.

I forced myself to create a mindset of success. This strange course of events, which may infuriate others, became my delight. I feel divinely inspired, a miracle forged from a simple and straightforward thought process. Whatever it was going to take, I would rouse in my son the spirit to progress beyond this moment. From within the tunnel I knew everything was going to be okay. I knew to tell my son not to worry, that I would turn all of our dreams into realities. I said this and never looked back to challenge the dreams.

One day at a time, we worked through doubt and fear. Each day, my son grew stronger. Each day I loved my son. Each day my son grew to love himself more. One challenge, empty rumors and idle chatter, we discarded as we refused to hear and focus on things irrelevant to the path we'd forged. A brilliant boy, misunderstood due to a handicap bestowed upon him by his surroundings. Focus the guide, we continued. Challenges continued, too. But we did not stop the positive flow and movements onward to victory. Together, we got through episodes of free-floating anxiety attacks.

After having been removed from school and court challenges, I would expect anyone would have bouts of anxiety. Having suffered through anxiety attacks as a teen, I knew the best way to deal with them was to embrace and encourage them, almost inviting them in.

I encouraged my son to journal his thoughts and feelings and work for others in a caring and helping capacity. I wanted him look to the future. We drove to Los Angeles to explore a variety of universities. We stayed at nice places in Laguna Beach and fully enjoyed the experience. I enrolled him into another school where the principal encouraged his academic performance. This school encouraged his ascension into advanced placement classes. My son started to talk, open up about who he was. He, who had been fearful of even eye contact, was becoming more comfortable with himself and others.

As soon as we were turning huge corners, my son healing and becoming secure within himself, my ex-husband commanded that my son move back into his home. The father continued to retain primary custody. My son was open to returning to his father's home as he had friends there and thought moving back to his school might not be so bad. Two days later, I received an urgent call: "Mom, I have to come back now." So began my son's mission to empower his mother. "Mom, wake up and fight for me. You are not fighting hard enough. Mom, you have to win." Perhaps you may be so empowered. Perhaps by a voice crying out. Or, perhaps, by a voice crying from within.

CHAPTER SIXTEEN

# Recovery, Restored Energy and Expectation

*The story "Tunnel Vision" concludes with a detailed accounting and "road map" of one individual's journey from violence to the creation of a healthy and prosperous future. Miracles and dreams are achieved for those who seek to dream, for those who are determined to shut out the noise, for those who learn how to focus, simplify, and clarify life. Join us in the creativity that "Tunnel Vision" brings; it is truly amazing for all who embrace the concept and are determined to live life fully with "Tunnel Vision" as their guide. Say what you really want and go for it! Embrace your dreams with a desire and passion that shuts out all question and negativity. Never stop. As my eldest son says, "Mom, you are not trying hard enough; try harder." We ask you to try harder. Live fully and enjoy every moment in peace.*

$S$ay what you want to say in this lifetime and go for it in an unwavering fashion. Embrace your dreams with a desire and passion that shuts out all question and negativity. Never ever stop once you are within the tunnel. The tunnel will protect, guide, and nurture your forward movement. Live fully and accept no less than the best from yourself each and every day. Embrace your uniqueness. Enjoy every moment in peace, health, and prosperity. You deserve no less.

With our voices united in coordinated sequences of dreams and actions, we forge paths to new beginnings. Dreams happen and become our reality. With every turn, we dream to accomplish for ourselves something that will teach our children that our past does not bind us. We dream again. Our children see the power in dreams and in miracles. Though we worship what was, we must move on, living life as the wind, flowing and moving in rhythm with the land. Flying as the birds, ever higher, and yet with inspiration, velocity, and navigation as our guides so as not to collide with others also aiming high. Those whose intention is to fly have no fear; they keep soaring.

Our time here is short, lessons we impart are ones learned and those yet to be discovered. I have come to a place of healing in my life where those around me are by my choice. They are intently focused on the creation of miracles. Whether they too came here out of a place of hurt, longing to find miracles I am not sure. All I know is the feeling of peace and youthfulness that surrounds me now. All I know is that I laugh with ease.

My eldest son's demands for peace and harmony within his life not only forced change for himself, they became compulsory for me to evolve as well. In a college essay, he spoke of "Sir Joshua," who slew the dragons to fight off fear and negativity. My son did this in a fairy tale, yet he was moving mountains to do the same in real life. No longer do we allow negativity to surround us. We do not allow it to intrude on our thoughts, words, and actions. Silver linings emerge when you view challenging events as opportunities.

The approach I speak of is not unique. It involves a disciplined and defined focus of words, actions, and thoughts every day and all the time. It is available for all who are ready and able to hear the inner voice and the dreams we express to others. Try to experience singing to yourself and playing music so loudly, it drowns out any inner voices of self-doubt and sorrow. If it does not work the first time, try again until it does. Never stop trying and play the music louder if you must. Disciplined restraint and control over all that is negative is required in your life from here forward.

The tunnel vision is the image used to create the boundaries. There is nothing that can get in the way of progress once you begin. Once inside the tunnel, you cannot stop nor move backward on your path. Only forward motion is allowed until your aim has been achieved. It involves standing straighter, speaking more clearly, and making positive things happen on a daily basis.

When speaking to others, you'll soon find you are an expert at knowing whether that person is on course or still caught in a negative pattern of words and actions. If the latter, silently pull away, as any association with negativity impedes your progress. You have the right to grieve for them as their immobility is costly. But you must move onward, not allowing yourself to get caught in their thought patterns and negative energy.

Move forward safely and securely within the tunnel, allowing your clarity to be your guide. Looking ahead, close your eyes and see the brightness ahead of you. Imagine this overwhelming brightness every day and embrace this healing thought, for it will save you.

Utilize knowledge, skills, values, and drive to achieve our wildest dreams. Speak, and it shall be done; believe and it shall be accomplished. But be careful what you wish for, as words clothed in focus are quite powerful if bound with belief as strong as the strongest of convictions. Look to the tallest of trees; be as they are. Allow your burning desire to create an energy never before imagined. If you are ready, every dream you have wished for will come your way.

Make a difference. Choose to care and dedicate yourself to listen to and be supportive of others. Never give up on another who may be dealing with tremendous loss. Help them to move forward as you have moved forward. Never assume you know what they went through; do not judge. Allow the tunnel to be your guiding light and assist in graciously directing others to see the benefit of tunnel vision as you do. There is not a minute to waste in providing a helping hand. The passage of time causes severe and long-term scarring. When we intervene immediately, we provide the opportunity for an enhanced chance of recovery. By nurturing an individual's present reality, chances of healing improve.

I strive to protect and nurture orphans left in cribs without adequate loving interaction and care. The little ones are conditioned early in life to believe their crying and tears will not bring the relief they seek. It is a learned behavior pattern and is maladaptive for them to grow and learn they are loved.

I cry out in hope of influencing this pattern of neglect and inadequate conditions rampant in orphanages around the world. Empowering one, I will hope to impact many by my actions. I move on to save the children. I came from a place of having all material things. But this was woefully incomplete. I learned this through pain.

Schools are too busy and have legal boundaries which do not allow them to examine closely the individual stories of abuse. There is no way for the teacher to know and correctly verify those children suffering from lack of attention or from verbal assaults. It becomes a sticky situation to reveal what is happening to outside agencies without instilling in the parent distrust for the school's intentions. By the time the child gets to high school, no one, not even the child, wants to mention whether an issue of abuse exists. For this child who has trouble achieving and concentrating, we must make ourselves question this rationale before the child remains lost forever.

Beyond my quest for orphans, I include myself in a growing list of visionaries who are creating sustainable farms. Funny, I was pensive to plant the first tree, first removing star thistles one by one, challenged by the abundance and variety of weeds, wanting a picture perfect canvas. What if it was not "right"? But I was encouraged by a friend to not fuss over design but to start planting. Go ahead and plant something. Anything! he would say. Now my farm is surrounded with two-hundred-plus olive trees, fig, plum, almond, and apple. David Austin rose bushes. I am overcome with the desire to nurture the earth where once I was afraid.

Learn more, be more, expect more of yourself in the

process of this lifetime. Delight in it, whatever the day brings for we must dig in the dirt before the flowers will grow. We must examine and enjoy life fully at every opportunity. Even the weeds can be beautiful! All things happen for a reason; there are lessons of patience, humility, and rationality presented to us every day. Perhaps someone needy has been alone and or deprived. Cherish in the moment and give. Take it in, processing all this and more with grace, style, and elegance. The pieces will fit together.

All of us at some point are tested by difficult times. Some of us choose to deal with the challenging times with a forward thrust of force so as to move mountains. Once our course of action begins, we at once know to love and believe in ourselves as those around us have done. In our own way, many of us come to a point in life where listening to self and love for self is the safest and most wonderful roadmap to our success. This road of happiness and accomplishment can take us away from negativity and violence. We listen to ourselves. We travel on, making dreams and commitments to self to enrich the earth that surrounds us. We love completely those who love us. We stop at nothing to create miracles.

We embrace our dreams.

# CHAPTER SEVENTEEN

# Choose to Make a Difference

*We welcome you and invite you to heal, to dream, and to
create miracles!*

*Quietly and miraculously maintain energy, health, and fo-
cus to enrich yourself and those around you with positive change.
It will happen. Believe me, I know.*

There are things in life best accomplished by giving totally to others. There is emotion shared which is embraced and
accepted with the care and the nurturing of another. We are
not to live our lives as islands. It is time to act, to move focus
from the pain and violence of the past. To embrace today,
tithing and sharing whatever gifts we can offer. I found myself,
after the loss of my children, online, intently focusing on the
many orphans in the world. At first, I thought I could adopt
every one. After careful consideration, I chose to sponsor orphans.

What I have gained in giving has returned to me power

and stamina beyond what I would have ever thought possible. I am in awe of the strength of people in pain to reach out and touch me. I can tell you to give, but these are only words. Once you do bestow of yourself, you will know and understand.

Think on it and pray on it. There is no shortage of people to help in this world. One orphanage I follow has no running water, no resources to aid those affected by the ravages of disease. Many who have known me a long time would look at my efforts with doubt and incredulousness. Natalia won't be in a position to assist with a mission like that! Ah, but they don't know how far we have come in such a short period of time with the promise of dreams and vision as our guide. They don't know the power of dreams, the power of tunnel vision.

It was my experience that had me gravitating towards orphans. I remember when my small children would dread being picked up by my ex-husband. Every exchange would involve fear and crying. Car doors were broken in the process, mental and physical scars were cast. There was never a calm point where spirits were recognized and love was shared. There was always violence. Small children were afraid to share love with me for fear of retaliation. They were made cautious and fearful about what to say to me and how to say it. It's a story painted with grief and sorrow. My children had to bear the tragedy. They never asked for this. They never asked to, in a sense, become orphans themselves. The silver lining was finding myself focused on the forward motion of assistance. Not just for myself and for my children, but for all orphans everywhere.

The journey has brought me towards the orphanage as well as to the courts, where I can, hopefully, provide an influence that was sorely missing for me during my family dealings. I have become a court-appointed mediator. From tragedy and pain come experience and with experience comes the responsibility to share it. Mediation can soften the sharp corners of a court system that fails to regard the value of each case, the value of each person.

Kids with no direction, essentially (or literally) orphaned, are open to trouble, often leading them to prison, or worse. Tragically, they are unlikely to break from their patterns. There is a seventy percent prison recidivism rate for such children.

Without the understanding of a teacher or a friend, prison becomes the unfortunate option. This is what the public defender did to my oldest son. This is the protocol. My son summoned the strength to break the pattern, but this is not so with most. Victimized children are the innocent ones whose lives are changed by violence and abandonment and parental indifference.

Many times, outward signs lie completely dormant until later when it emerges that these children lack normal development and coping skills. Attention to the cues and signals of children crying out silently in pain must be understood immediately by professionals and caretakers alike before it is too late for action.

It is a dream, but dreams can be fulfilled one person at a time. One orphan at a time. Or one orphanage at a time. Pick your cause. Make a difference. Somehow. By pulling those around you up, you pull yourself up as well.

Moving forward now as if in perfect order, I completed my first year of law school, mastery of law is both an honor and an opportunity. I struggle with cutbacks in the hospital. But I breathe, and know that all will be okay. I have my sons whom I adore. Funny to look back as nothing that bothered me so greatly then is even a consideration now. I remember well my ex-husband declaring that I would never be successful in law. With Tunnel Vision in place, we eliminate the negative influences. I embrace only positive influences around me. And as for my ex, he has stopped yelling completely.

My neighbors the Turoni's are very much in love. Together they embrace the changes in life together in this small valley place. I choose to surround myself with beauty – both in nature, and in the people I associate with. For in the people is displayed the passion of life. Whatever your story, come to realize your resourcefulness and understand the endless opportunities that await you in this lifetime. I have grown by challenging myself to dream big and accomplish much. I challenge you to move past adversity to find the silver linings in all things.

Look for good always and as Cedric would say, "Fight Mom, 'cause you are not fighting hard enough Mom…Slay the dragon." Be crystal clear with your vision of your future as you see it. Write about it, take photographs, allow the lessons you have learned to permeate another person's glory. This will connect you to others, be of love much more careful than anything.

For in the connections in life we heal. Allow your dreams to paint your world! So allow yourself to trust, take a stand, be passionate, make a difference, crazy as it may seem. I have and did and will continue to live life as if each day were my last.

Go for it!

CPSIA information can be obtained at www.ICGtesting.com
Printed in the USA
BVOW07s1605250215

389317BV00001B/1/P